CLASSIC RACING CARS

THE POST-WAR FRONT-ENGINED GP CARS

CLASSIC RACING CARS

THE POST-WAR FRONT-ENGINED GP CARS

NYE & GODDARD

Foulis

Haynes
®

A **Foulis** Motoring Book

First published 1991

Published by:
Haynes Publishing Group
Sparkford, Nr Yeovil
Somerset BA22 7JJ, England

Haynes Publications Inc
861 Lawrence Drive, Newbury Park,
California 91320, USA

A catalogue record for this book is available
from the British Library

ISBN 0 85429 775 8

Library of Congress Catalog Card Number
91–71117

Editor: Robin Read
Design & Layout: Mike King
Typeset in Times Med Rom 11/12 pt and
printed in England by J. H. Haynes & Co.
Ltd.

CONTENTS

PREFACE

Most enthusiasts are very familiar with the general shape of motor racing history at its top level. You will already know how there was virtual free-Formula racing in the immediate postwar years, followed by a cobbled together Formula from 1948 combining the best surviving elements of the pre-war classes. You will know how the 2½-litre Formula reigned for seven seasons 1954-60, then gave way to the tiny little kiddy-car 1500cc Formula, eventually leading into the 3-litre Formula 1 and the modern age of rear-engined racing. The accent since then has been increasingly upon ever more modern purpose-built autodrome circuits, a massively exposed 16-strong GP series televized worldwide, aerospace-style engineering, huff, puff and general glitz as money and commercial prestige has come to count for everything.

In these pages we are looking back at a rather more gentle, and certainly more genteel, age of motor racing in which the private owner could still compete against the big batallions. The circuits upon which they raced owed their shape more to local geography than to any man-made regulations, and the cars themselves were somehow more substantial. They might also have been generally less sophisticated, primitive sometimes, misconceived quite often, but almost without exception possessing a special charm and nostalgic attraction of their own.

These were the cars built during the final phase of the front-engined Grand Prix car's long, long reign. What we have tried to do here is to present a concise and easily digestible view of both these cars and their period – a glimpse of the bygone days of a great sport-cum-promotional business the way it used to be. The emphasis has been upon presenting hitherto unpublished photographs or reproducing some which you may have seen before but never so extensively captioned as part of a continuing narrative. Where some marques or models have been particularly well covered in other publications, we have generally set them aside in favour of more unusual fare. Of course, there will be omissions but any you may recognise have been very carefully chosen from a short-list photo selection extending far beyond four figures. So what follows presents some well-known shapes, some familiar faces, some little-known cars and some very obscure names – each one having contributed in some way to the fascinating story of the postwar front-engined Grand Prix car.

Doug Nye & Geoff Goddard

INTRODUCTION

Emile Levassor set the trend. His company Panhard & Levassor was introduced to the newly-developed lightweight, high speed internal combustion engine way back in the dark ages of motoring. The veteran Stuttgart engineer Gottlieb Daimler, who had developed the most efficient automotive internal combustion engine then in existence, had granted the French manufacturing rights to a young Belgian patent lawyer friend of his named Edouard Sarazin.

Sarazin was also an old friend of Emile Levassor, and when he died prematurely on Christmas Eve, 1887, his Daimler manufacturing rights passed to his widow, Louise, who subsequently married the Panhard man.

Daimler came to think as highly of Levassor as he had previously of Sarazin and, on February 17 1890, the first Panhard & Levassor car clattered away from the company's Parisian machine-tool factory. It was powered, of course, by a Daimler patent engine.

This Levassor-designed prototype carried its engine amidships, adjacent to the chain-driven rear wheels as was standard at that pioneering time. However, through the mid-summer of 1891 as the first potential customers began to show serious interest, Levassor redesigned his product to carry its engine at the front. He aimed to diminish the mechanical vibration transmitted to the soft road springs. They had to be soft to insulate the driver and his passenger(s) from the battering meted out by the normal rough roads of the period.

This forward mounting of the engine was not in itself new. Bollée had already sited his steam engines up front in his horseless carriages, but where the extreme flexibility of steam had given his power units maximum torque at stall, Levassor's Daimler-patent internal combustion engine was effectively a constant-speed device which simply sat there clattering away continuously at some 600-800 rpm.

The car's driveline to its rear wheels was then interrupted by a gearbox, whose various ratios enabled the vehicle to drag itself away from rest, to cruise on the flat, rush down hills – "rush" being a relative term you understand – and to crawl up hills. The driver used the gearbox simply to adjust his road speed by ker-unching it from gear to gear while the engine maintained constant rpm. Levassor's great line *"C'est brutal mais ça marche"* – "It's brutal, but it goes" has often been quoted. It was deadly accurate.

This automotive geography – engine up front, gearbox behind it, driving to the rear wheels while leaving the front wheels free to steer – became accepted throughout the industry as the *Système Levassor*.

Within these precepts established by Emile Levassor, the classical front-engined road-going motor car had been born, while in parallel with its development there evolved the classical front-engined racing car.

Grand Prix Racing

Grand Prix racing was founded in 1906 as the premier form of road-circuit competition, with entry lists open to teams of no more than three cars each from any manufacturer. France was very much the centre not only of the world's burgeoning motor industry but also of adequately organised motoring competition. Its *Automobile Club de France* had established effective international dominance through being the first to be formed, and its Competitions Committee had developed the open-to-all Grand Prix race format in response to the only preceding literally "Inter-National" form of racing which had been embodied in the pioneer Gordon Bennett Cup series.

In that brief (and in truth poorly-supported) competition, the famous proprietor of the *New York Herald* newspaper had launched an event to be contested on equal terms between teams selected to represent the cream of their national industries. Right from its inception in 1900, this format deeply irritated the French. Their indigenous motor industry was by far the world's largest and most diverse. However, Gordon Bennett rules allowed no more than three cars to each competing nation's team, thus preventing many otherwise interested manufacturers from competing.

The French argued that, with the largest industry, they should be allowed the largest team. After 1904, therefore, they gave due warning that they would abandon support for the Gordon

Bennett event and establish their own effectively free-entry Grand Prix instead.

This new event was first run, very successfully, near Le Mans in 1906. Its annual repetition on a variety of French circuits subsequently became the single greatest motor sport event of each year.

A new set of regulations governing construction and specification of eligible cars was formulated each season by the ACF committee, and it was not until after the First World War that Grand Prix Formulae were agreed internationally – (effectively in Europe). They provided stable requirements intended to apply for more than one year. In addition, more national Grand Prix races were added to the annual calendar. The original *Grand Prix de l'Automobile Club de France* – loosely known as the French Grand Prix – was joined in 1921 by the *Gran Premio d'Italia* at Brescia (later repeated regularly at Monza). In 1925 the *Grand Prix de Belgique* was instituted at Spa-Francorchamps. In 1926 the RAC Grand Prix of Great Britain was first run at Brooklands and the *Grosser Preis von Deutschland* at AVUS, Berlin. In 1929 the inaugural *Grand Prix de Monaco* was run. Other premier-Formula races of major significance also filled the calendar, such as the San Sebastian Grand Prix in the Basque region of northwestern Spain from 1923 and the *Grand Prix de la Marne* at Reims-Gueux from 1925.

For such events of major Grand Prix status, a maximum engine capacity limit of 2-litres was applied from 1922-5. For 1926-7 this top limit was reduced to 1½-litres, and then as needs must when economy measures demand, an increasingly free *Formule Libre* class of anything-goes racing took over from 1928 and on through the Great Depression years of the early-1930s.

By 1932 it became clear that a degree of financial stability was returning. However, free-Formula racing had encouraged companies like Bugatti, Alfa Romeo and Maserati to build some hefty, effectively multiple-engined Grand Prix cars which were by general consent too fast both for their tyres and common-sense safety. The governing competitions committee of the International governing body of the period between the wars – the AIACR (*L'Association Internationale des Automobiles Clubs Reconnus*) – considered a more restrictive Grand Prix Formula which applied for three seasons from 1934 to 1936.

As the twin-engined Alfa Romeo *Tipo A* and the 16-cylinder Maserati *Tipo V4* had been so heavy, law-makers of the AIACR decided that a new maximum weight limit of – say – 750kg (1,653.45lbs) would correct the situation. This maximum weight limitation was to be verified by weighing the cars dry of fuel and oil, without tyres and driver. The general consensus at that time amongst the bureaucratic law-makers in Paris, was that such a Formula should effectively confine Grand Prix car engines to less than 3-litres and bridle power to around 250-275 horsepower and little more.

In double quick time, history proved the AIACR committee to have been hopelessly short-sighted.

Their 750kg maximum-weight Formula of 1934-6 provided the umbrella under which the new Mercedes-Benz and Auto Union teams from Germany, backed financially and in propaganda by Hitler's emergent Nazi State, established totally new standards of power and sheer, petrifying, blistering performance.

Using advanced technology, state-of-the-art lightweight metallurgy and all the logical tenacity so characteristic of German industry they introduced all-independently suspended multi-cylinder supercharged Grand Prix cars. They punched engine size way out towards 6-litres, power close to 650bhp, and lap records to previously unimagined speeds by the time this '750kg Formula', extended for one final season through 1937, finally lapsed.

When the AIACR came to consider a replacement Formula for 1938-40 they decided upon a split-equivalency class, judging (under pressure from France in particular) that a supercharged car with engine capacity restricted to no more than 3-litres, should approximately match the performance of an unsupercharged car enjoying 50 per cent greater swept volume, a maximum of 4½-litres.

The German teams took the supercharged road to produce ultimately two-stage supercharged 3-litre cars whose speed between refuelling stops put them well beyond the reach of even the fastest unblown 4½-litre car, even if one should achieve the fuel economy to survive a Grand Prix distance non-stop.

During these years between the wars, the ancient front-engined *Système Levassor* had, meanwhile, been abandoned by two Grand Prix constructors; Benz as early as 1923, and then far more significantly by Ferdinand Porsche's *P-Wagen* project which became the Auto Union 16-cylinder series of cars of 1934-7.

Using this series as its basis for continuing rear-engined Grand Prix car development, Auto Union's later Chief Engineer Robert Eberan von Eberhorst then developed his far more effective and more stable de Dion rear-suspended V12 mid-engined *Typ* D 3-litre supercharged cars for 1938-9.

By the time that the outbreak of the Second World War called a halt to Grand Prix Formula racing – the last race being run in Belgrade, Yugoslavia on Sunday, 3 September 1939 – the smooth-riding, good-handling Auto Union D-Type was showing serious signs of toppling Mercedes-Benz's front-engined ascendancy. This superiority had brought the Stuttgart team consecutive European Championship titles in the years 1937-9.

Among the unsupercharged $4\frac{1}{2}$-litre opposition so consistently crushed by these well-funded, technologically-advanced German teams, the French Talbots and Delahayes had featured most prominently. Several manufacturers interested in racing had abandoned any serious pretensions to fully-fledged Grand Prix competition, in favour of the subsidiary $1\frac{1}{2}$-litre supercharged class for *Voiturettes* – the Formula 2 or Formula 3000 of its day.

This class division was rooted way back in racing antiquity – pre-1900. Motoring pioneer Leon Bollée is credited with having coined the term to describe his three-wheeler of 1895. 'Voiturette' later became common currency to describe small-capacity cars in France. The first *Voiturette* competition class was formalized for under 400kg cars (644lbs) in the Paris-Amsterdam-Paris race of 1898.

Most of the great city-to-city races of that Heroic Age included *Voiturette* classes, and also an intermediate division for *Voitures Legères* – light cars – which had to weigh between 400 and 650kg (644lbs to 1046lbs).

Many of history's most enterprising marques won their spurs racing through these smaller classes. Peugeot, Hispano-Suiza, Delage and Sunbeam were the most prominent of these new constructors. From 1906-10 the *Coupe de l'Auto* provided the *Voiturette* world with its most important prize while similar events like the Catalan and Sicilian Cup races were also well supported.

From 1911 to 1914, *Voiturette* regulations permitted 3-litre capacity engines and the class attracted some superb, advanced engineering from Vauxhall, Sunbeam and Peugeot. These

were extremely effective racing cars, witness Rigal's Sunbeam *Voiturette* finishing third overall amongst the giants in the 1912 Grand Prix.

Through the 1920s, as small 2-litre and then 1500cc cars fully assumed Grand Prix status, *Voiturette* racing disappeared as a separate class and the term itself became obsolescent.

But then, during the Depression years as *Formule Libre* effectively assumed Grand Prix status, a series of subsidiary 1100-1500cc races were held which effectively revived the old 'little car' class of competition.

They were known, once again, as *Voiturette* events, and earned widespread acceptance through 1931-3. In comparative terms there were plenty of suitable cars around, while many enthusiastic young men – and women – were sufficiently interested and wealthy to enter and drive them. In addition a number of smaller factories could afford to provide the technical back-up to ensure the viability of the class. Race organisers throughout Europe also recognised the chance to run inexpensive races which could attract strong entries and provide the paying public with adequate entertainment.

When the new 750kg maximum weight Grand Prix Formula was applied for 1934, up-to-1500cc *Voiturette* racing was formally accepted by the AIACR as the next step down the ladder. It was thus formalized as a true predecessor to the Formula 2 equivalent of the late-1940s, the 1950s, and throughout the early 1980s.

This subsidiary $1\frac{1}{2}$-litre class thrived from 1934-9, and as peace settled over Europe in 1945-6, the surviving stock of usable pure-bred racing cars was mostly pre-war 1500cc *Voiturettes*. The few usable 3-litres supercharged and $4\frac{1}{2}$-litres unsupercharged Grand Prix cars of 1938-9 vintage were relatively rare. The all-conquering German Grand Prix cars of the 1930s had been scattered to the winds by war and in any case the understandable vindictiveness of French political interests prevented German entry to the postwar motor racing fraternity until 1950.

It was therefore logical to promote a stop-gap, monoposto class for the recovery years. This implied a mixture of $1\frac{1}{2}$-litre supercharged *Voiturettes* and $4\frac{1}{2}$-litre unsupercharged Grand Prix cars which was not a bad match. Although the ultimate developments of the 1500cc line would prove to be extremely fast hares, the grumbling $4\frac{1}{2}$-litre cars could occasionally prove their non-stop tortoise tactics to be a recipe for success.

Farina – Alfa Romeo 158 – Geneva, 1946

THE RACING BEGINS

THE FRONT-ENGINED GP CARS

1945

RACING RETURNS...

At the end of World War 2, Europe was largely devastated. Motor racing was a costly and complex sport to revive. Support and permits were required from all manner of local bureaucrats and police authorities. Roads had to be closed for an event to be run. Fuel supplies had to be arranged – no easy task amid the privations of immediate post-war times – and above all the needs of spectator crowds had to be met. Paradoxically, these crowds were going to be immense, because the public in almost every European state had been totally starved of genuine sporting spectacle for six long years. There was a ravenous appetite throughout the Continent for sporting entertainment and the chance to forget.

When European hostilities finally ceased in May 1945, followed by the end of the Pacific war that August, motor racing was quick to resume, suitably by courtesy of the French.

The first peacetime race meeting to be organised was the *Coupe de Paris*, held in the Bois de Boulogne, the Hyde Park of Paris, on 9 September 1945. A 2.8km (1.74-mile) parkland road circuit was chosen, and the programme included races for motor-cycles and sidecars in 250, 350, 500 and 600cc classes, followed by three events for cars.

They were a 36-lap, up to 1500 cc race for the *Coupe Robert Benoist*; the 36-lap, 1501-3000cc *Coupe de la Libération*, and the 43-lap, over-3000cc *Coupe des Prisonniers*.

This meeting was organised by the AGACI and the GNRM in aid of *La Campagne Nationale du Retour*. AGACI was the *Association Française des Coureurs en Automobile* – The French Association of Motor Racers – while the *Groupement National des Refractaires et Maquisards* was a national association of former Resistance fighters. Proceeds from the meeting were to help fund the early repatriation of French deportees and PoWs, thousands of whom still languished in DP (displaced person) camps and holding centres throughout Europe.

Other than its post-WW2 primacy, this meeting holds little sporting significance, but it did set the shape for events to come. For France in general and for Parisians in particular, it was also a hugely emotional symbol of newfound freedom and caring enthusiasm. It rekindled the French love of *monoplace* motor racing, bruised pre-war by German dominance and totally suppressed since 1939.

Right: September 9 1945 – The *Coupe des Prisonniers*, Bois de Boulogne, Paris. Jean-Pierre Wimille headed the winners in Europe's first postwar motor race meeting, here in the feature race of this *Coupes de Paris* meeting. His car is the unique 4.7-litre Bugatti *monoplace* sprint car – chassis '50180' – built in 1939. It did not comply with the Grand Prix Formula, since it used the *Type* 50B supercharged engine, way over the Grand Prix Formula's blown 3-litre limit. At least it had, by 1939 standards, a modern if bulky body design, and hydraulic rather than mechanical brakes. In 1939 Wimille had driven it to second FTDs at La Turbie and Prescott hill-climbs. He had also won the *Coupe de Paris* at Montlhéry at over 85 mph, so here in the Hyde Park of Paris he could claim to have scored his second consecutive victory in the event, after five years of destructive war.

Eugéne Mauve, the pre-war organiser of the 24-Hour *Bol d'Or* races, arranged it all, with Maurice Henry and the doyen of racing journalists, Charles Faroux, as Race Directors. In the race-programme Henry wrote an impassioned tribute to his late friend, the great pre-war French Champion driver Robert Benoist.

A leading *Maquisard*, Benoist had been flown to London and then parachuted back into France in 1944 in preparation for the invasion. He was reputedly betrayed and arrested by the Gestapo in the Panthéon quarter of Paris on 7 June 1944 – D-Day plus 1.

He was deported to Germany on August 8 agonisingly close to liberation, and there was executed in Buchenwald on 14 September 1944:

Right: Bois de Boulogne, Paris – The *Coupe des Prisonniers* field booms away from the start with the sports Talbot T150C of 'Levegh' (Pierre Bouillon, race number 6), leading Philippe Étancelin's Alfa Romeo *Monza* (3), Louis Gérard's Maserati 8CM (4), Raymond Sommer's Talbot-Lago *Monoplace Centrale* 1939 Grand Prix car (centre) and Georges Grignard's Delahaye (14). Wimille, having arrived too late for practice, is hidden at the back of the grid. The Bois was packed by a massive crowd which greeted the racers with immense enthusiasm. This meeting confirmed that peace had been restored at long last.

just 51 weeks before the Bois de Boulogne race was run to commemorate his name.

There, Amedée Gordini won the Benoist Cup at 59mph in his 1100cc Simca-Fiat special. With so many cars being held over for the main race, the up to 3-litre event then "fell a bit flat", as one reporter put it, Henri Louveau's Maserati winning easily at 61mph. Sixteen cars then packed the narrow grid for the main event. Raymond Sommer led the opening lap in a GP Talbot-Lago before Jean-Pierre Wimille – who had not practised – rapped ahead in the 4.7 Bugatti *monoplace* which had climbed England's Prescott hill in 1939. He won at nearly 71mph, after lapping at over 78 mph. Postwar motor racing had recommenced. Since then it has continued unbroken to this day. The breed of front-engined Grand Prix cars, however, survived only until 1961.

1946
A FULL YEAR'S FORMULE LIBRE

Into the first full year of peace since 1938, pre-war cars filled the grids of the relatively few races run to *Formule Libre*, free-Formula, meaning in effect that anything looking remotely like a racing car was acceptable for competition. The important thing, in the organisers' eyes, was merely to stage a race, take admission money from the public, distribute start and prize money to the participants, and hopefully pocket the profit.

Before World War 1, international motor racing had been dominated by the patrician *Automobile Club de France*, with its headquarters flanking the palatial Place de la Concorde in Paris. As sporting ambitions and activity had mushroomed in other countries so other national sporting bodies had been founded, such as the Royal Automobile Club of Great Britain & Ireland – the RACGBI – in London, and the *Reale Automobile Club d'Italia* – the RACI – in Rome. These national bodies each sent delegates to an ACF-dominated International governing body, based in the Place de la Concorde under the title *L'Association International des Automobiles Clubs Reconnus* – The International Association of

Recognized Automobile Clubs – the AIACR. Motor racing matters were then controlled by this body's subsidiary *Commission Sportive International* – the CSI.

These International bodies were revived post-war, and it was in 1946 that the AIACR by common consent adopted the less cumbersome title still current today, the *Fedération International de l'Automobile* – The International Automobile Federation – or FIA.

The immediate question facing this body's sporting commission in 1946 was to arrive at a universally acceptable Formula to govern re-emergent single-seater racing. Initially, it presented little problem. There was only one answer – *Formule Libre*, catering for any surviving pre-war racing cars which factories or private owners might care to run, but all competing cars had to burn alcohol fuel.

The ingredients of the fuel brews burned by racing cars of that period were not too difficult to obtain. However, provision of normal-grade petrol to propel spectators to the race meeting was quite another matter. Petrol rationing, or even a total ban on its use for leisure, was widespread and endemic.

Consequently, organisers preferred race circuits sited within cities to attract an audience able to attend on foot or by bus and tram. During the 1946 racing season, 15 major Formula races were held in Europe, of which 11 were in France, two in Italy, one in Switzerland, and one in formerly neutral Spain.

The French race meetings were concentrated in the unscathed south and around Paris, which had escaped the bombardment that had flattened so many northern cities. They followed the urban street or parkland circuit pattern in Nice, Marseilles, the Bois de Boulogne, St Cloud, Perpignan, Dijon, Nantes and – a rare northern venue – Lille while a more rural road circuit was adopted outside St Just-sur-Loire at Forez. In the southern Midi the Tarnside *Les Planques* road course outside Albi was also revived.

Two Parisian race meetings were held in the Bois de Boulogne, one headed by the *Coupe de la Résistance* on May 30, and the other by the *Grand Prix du Salon* which coincided with the first postwar Paris Motor Show on October 3. The great *Grand Prix des Nations* was held round the wide boulevards of Geneva, while the Italian *Gran Premio del Valentino* took place in Turin's riverside Valentino Park on September 1. It was followed by the *Gran Premio di Milano* in Sempione Park on September 23. The one major Spanish event was the revived Peña Rhin GP over the Pedralbes boulevard circuit in Barcelona on October 27.

An entire flotilla of pre-war Maseratis re-emerged to do battle with mainly sports-based Delahaye *Type* 135 variants, a handful of Talbot-Lagos and a smattering of obsolescent Bugattis. Most significantly the wealthy French ace Raymond Sommer emerged as proud owner-driver of a 1938 3-litre straight-8 engined Alfa Romeo 308 Grand Prix car.

It was the only representative of the formerly dominant supercharged 3-litre Grand Prix class to face the unblown $4\frac{1}{2}$s and 1500cc supercharged *Voiturettes*, yet the cultivated skills of Luigi Villoresi beat Sommer's panache when racing first resumed on the seafront at Nice on 22 April 1946.

At Marseilles on the *Boulevard du Prado* course Sommer turned the tables on the visiting Italians, but this time he was driving a Maserati 4CL, not the beefy Alfa. He won again at Forez, and then Jean-Pierre Wimille – merely an emergent talent pre-war, now fast becoming the standard setter of his day, fielded the 308 in the Bois de Boulogne to dominate the *Coupe de la Résistance*.

Sommer responded by winning at St Cloud after hasty preparation robbed the Alfa Corse factory team from Milan of a first-time victory on their postwar début with two 1939-40 *Tipo* 158s, although 'Nino' Farina set fastest lap in one.

J-P Wimille then restored Alfa's honour with consecutive victories in the next two race meetings at the wheel of his Tipo 308, at Perpignan on June 30 and the following weekend at Dijon.

One week later, on July 14, the Albi Grand Prix was revived and the crowd stood in silent tribute to the late Johnny Wakefield, winner of the 1939 event, killed flying with the Royal Navy's Fleet Air Arm. Reg Parnell drove what had been Wakefield's Maserati 4CL in the race, facing such superstars as Nuvolari and Villoresi. The legendary Tazio Nuvolari won and followers felt that postwar motor racing had got into its stride at last.

Alfa Corse re-emerged in Geneva for the *Grand Prix des Nations*, fielding a full team of four 158 *Alfetta* cars, for Farina, Achille Varzi – Nuvolari's equally legendary pre-war rival, now rehabilitated after years of morphine dependency – Count Carlo Felice Trossi and their invited French guest driver, J-P Wimille, fast on his way to becoming the leading driver of those postwar, pre-World Championship days.

They faced a flock of Maseratis and British-entered ERAs, and the race was simply no contest. This time the Alfa Corse cars were properly prepared. They swept all opposition aside. Farina won from Trossi and Wimille with Nuvolari in fourth place after ramming Wimille intentionally in protest at what he considered to be the Frenchman's intentional baulking! Villoresi crashed and broke a leg.

'Raph' – the Marquis Raphael de Bethenod de las Casas – drove his Maserati 4CL to victory at Nantes after Wimille's Alfa 308 faltered. Sommer/Henri Louveau shared the 4CL which won at Lille, and on September 1 the *Gran Premio Valentino* in Turin's riverside park marked the return of real motor racing to Italian soil. Varzi won, for Alfa Romeo, winning again three weeks later in Heat One of the Milan Grand Prix, where factory test driver Consalvo Sanesi won Heat Two and Count Trossi the Final – all for Alfa Corse.

It was left to Maserati 4CLs to win the final events of the season, Sommer taking the *Grand Prix du Salon* in the Bois de Boulogne while Pelassa headed a woefully thin field in the revived Peña Rhin Grand Prix at Barcelona.

In Britain, meanwhile, postwar restrictions had confined motor sport largely to the sprint and hill-climb scene, although in Ireland the Ulster Trophy was run on a public road course outside Ballyclare where 'B.Bira' won narrowly in his cousin Prince Chula's ERA from Parnell's Maserati. Reg Parnell – the rough-hewn Derbyshire farmer and haulier – confided to friends he had drawn alongside 'Bira' at least a dozen times but was every time denied space to pass. He did not protest, but the message was understood. Pre-war ways and tugging one's forelock to the titled classes were both now history.

THE CARS COMPETING 1946

Alfa Romeo *Tipo* 158, 308 and 8C-2300 Monza; Amilcar; Alta; Bugatti *Type* 35; Cisitalia D46; Delage *Grand Prix* and D670; Delahaye 135; ERA A-Type, B-Type and E-Type; Maserati 4CL, 6CM and 8C-3000; Salmson; Talbot-Platé *Grand Prix Speciale*; Talbot-Lago *Monoplace 1938* and *1939*, *Type* 26C and T150C *Speciale*.

Opposite top: 22 April 1946 – *Grand Prix de Nice* – Opening race of the first full postwar season of International motor racing. Luigi Villoresi won here in a *Scuderia Milano* Maserati 4CL, heading a field ranging from 4CLs to 3½-litre sports Delahayes and elderly Bugattis. Paul Friderich's sports V12 Delahaye was not allowed to start, enabling the event to be run as a scratch race, rather than on handicap. An estimated 50,000 spectators attended. One coming man they saw was Robert Mazaud, seen cornering here his immaculately-presented 4CL. He had driven Delahayes immediately pre-war, but emerged as one of the fastest – if rather wild – French drivers of 1946. He retired here with reported magneto trouble after featuring strongly, but later won Heat One at Marseilles, was third at St Cloud, and then tackled the 185.5km (115ml) *Grand Prix des 24 Heures du Mans* on an appallingly narrow and bumpy circuit at Nantes. On the third lap he lost control of his 4CL which rolled and threw him out, Eugéne Chaboud crashing his Delahaye 135 in avoidance. Mazaud died; becoming the first fatality in postwar motor racing.

Left: 21 July 1946 – *Grand Prix des Nations*, Geneva – The greatest of pre-war Champions, Tazio Nuvolari, was reckoned by none less than Rudi Uhlenhaut, chief engineer of the mighty Daimler-Benz *Rennabteilung* to be in decline by 1938, when he was already 46 years old. True or not, he still won Grands Prix for Auto Union in both that year and 1939, and reappeared here six years later at the age of 54. He drove his *Scuderia Milano* Maserati 4CL to lead the Nice Grand Prix in April, until valve trouble intervened. He won at Albi on 14 July but collapsed immediately afterwards, a developing respiratory disease forcing him to wear a face mask to filter the fumes from hot oil and alcohol fuel. Here in Geneva he finished third behind two *Alfettas* in Heat One, and fourth behind three of them in the Final, proving himself and his 4CL 'the best of the rest'. The folded aero screen and face visor combined maximum flow of clean, breathable air with visibility, allowing him to inhale without gagging in the airstream.

Above: Grand Prix des Nations again – Farina's *Alfetta*, the right-side of its radiator grille partially blanked off and colour-coded to aid recognition from the pits, dropping down through the gears into the Workers' Monument corner opposite the League of Nations building on the lakeside. Maserati 6CM and 4CL follow, freshly lapped. The four factory Alfa Romeos were in a class of their own, particularly the Farina, Varzi and Wimille cars which used the latest two-stage supercharged engines delivering *circa* 260 bhp. In contrast the earlier single-stage unit retained in Trossi's fourth 158 developed some 225 bhp at 7500 rpm. Here they began the run of success which remained virtually unbroken until the British Grand Prix of July 1951. Farina is about to win both his Heat and the Final, leading home team-mates Trossi and Wimille – the French ace third after a tangle with Nuvolari which cost him a lap and an Italian tongue-lashing.

17

Far left inset: Grand Prix des Nations – There'll always be an also-ran; in this case Max Christen, in his special-bodied and rather 'Alfa Romeo'-looking Maserati, displaying its red and white Swiss livery on home soil. Christen started at the back of the grid of Heat Two. He finished tenth and last and did not qualify for the Final. Yet, as always, they also serve . . .

Left inset: Grand Prix des Nations – Another Maserati also-ran. One of the most obscure of all Grand Prix car drivers, the Maserati privateer Vojtechovsky whose *Tipo* 6CM retired during Geneva's Heat One, his elderly road-plated car having at least provided an unusual patch of colour, silver and blue we believe. Do you know more?

Main picture: Grand Prix des Nations – More colour from one of the most colourful of all postwar racing drivers, Harry O'Reilly Schell is seen here during practice for the Geneva race in which his Maserati 6CM developed mechanical trouble and did not start its Heat. Harry's father, Laurie Schell, had founded the pre-war *Écurie Bleue* team of Delahaye long-distance sports and Grand Prix cars together with his formidable American wife, Lucy. When Laurie was killed in a road accident, Lucy O'Reilly Schell took over *Écurie Bleue* and ran it effectively up to the war. Here in Geneva 1946 her son's Maserati wears American white and blue, complete with stars and stripes (curiously reversed), and the *Écurie L.O.R. Schell* logo. He would go far as a works Formula 1 driver for Maserati, Vanwall and BRM before losing his life in a practice crash at Silverstone in 1960, while driving a Yeoman Credit/BRP team Cooper.

Grand Prix des Nations – British was not always best, even when driven by such a fearlessly committed hard tryer as George Abecassis. Despite his exotic surname, George was very much an Englishman, a former public schoolboy and lifelong car buff. Pre-war, he had taken a small filling station at Cranford (near today's Heathrow Airport) to finance his racing. In 1937 he bought the wreck of this single-seat all-independently sprung Alta in which Philip Jucker had been killed on the Isle of Man. Constructor Geoffrey Taylor charged £425 less the price of the wreckage to rebuild it as new and deliver it to George ready-to-run at Brooklands on Easter Monday 1938. He promptly burst straight into the headlines with it and by 1939 the Abecassis Alta was a genuine front-runner until badly damaged in a collision at Albi. Postwar, George reappeared in the now green reconstituted Alta, as here in Geneva, where he finished sixth in Heat One but retired from the Final. Suspension was by coil-springs, the hubs carried on vertical sliders mounted upon two cross-tubes – chassis number '61IS'.

Opposite top: 10 August 1946 – Ulster Trophy, Ballyclare – Road racing returned to the British Isles for the first time postwar as the Ulster AC strove to prove to HM Government that racing could be run on public roads without great risk to the spectating public. Contemporary feeling was that an accident-free meeting could speed revival of the Tourist Trophy. Two events were run on a 6.5km (4ml) circuit, an individual handicap and a 1500cc scratch race. 'Bira' won the latter in Chula's ERA 'R3B' *Romulus*, just holding off Parnell's ex-Johnny Wakefield pre-war Maserati 4CL, tail-wagging wildly here on the final corner of the final lap. Parnell told friends the Prince had baulked him deliberately throughout the closing stages, while Chula declared his cousin had been struggling to hold the ERA 'down the camber' on Ballyclare's narrow country roads . . .

Below: 23 September 1946 – Milan Grand Prix, Sempione Park – Alfa Romeo dominated their home Grand Prix. Here at the start of Heat One, the *Alfetta* pair driven by Varzi (2) and Trossi (12) take off on their way to a 1-2 finish, Heat Two confirming this as the overall result. Englishman Leslie Brooke's ERA 'R7B' is standing tall to the left of the head of the official in plus-fours (left); bluff, tough 'Brookie' finishing eighth in this Heat. Interestingly, the starter's (chequered) flag is still raised on the extreme right but they're rushing off regardless!

3 October 1946 – *Grand Prix du Salon*, Bois de Boulogne, Paris – Strolling along with an independent air – at least where their front suspension is concerned – are two more of the ubiquitous Maserati 4CLs, in this case the *Écurie Naphtra Corse* car driven by 'Raph' en route to second place overall behind Sommer's winning Scuderia Milano-entered version, and Henri Louveau in the second Milano car which eventually finished fourth. Maserati had introduced the *Tipo* 4CL in April 1939, nine apparently being completed – chassis '1564' to '1572' including the 1939 Tripoli streamliner later converted into a 6CM – before the outbreak of war that September. Italian forces were not in combat

until June 1940. One more – '1573' – seems to have been completed during the war, while another five – '1579' to '1583' – are listed for 1946, and eight more – '1584' to '1591' – followed in 1947. The final number credited to the 4CL series was '1592', supplied to Giuseppe Farina with a 4CLT two-stage supercharged engine in April 1948.

27 October 1946 – Peña Rhin Grand Prix, Barcelona, Spain – The much-travelled Leslie Brooke (6) more prominent this time, only narrowly beaten off the starting line by Luigi Villoresi's Maserati 4CL (in the centre). Also in 4CLs are Reg Parnell (second from right), the ultimately victorious Giorgio Pelassa and the equally unfamiliar Ciro Basadonna, Alberto Puigpalu and Arialdo Ruggeri. Just behind Villoresi's right shoulder is Raymond de Saugé's little Fiat 1100-engined Cisitalia D46 of the series-production type which did wonders for small-capacity single-seater 'circus' racing in Europe in these immediate postwar years.

1947

ITALY ON TOP...

Postwar motor racing really resumed its proper stride during this season as the Pau, Swiss, Belgian and Italian Grands Prix were revived, the latter in Milan's Sempione Park as its old spiritual home at Monza remained devastated by years of military use.

The Alfa Romeo 158s were campaigned as a full factory team, the only one in European motor racing at that time. It was a works team whose mechanical and logistical might, plus sheer driving talent within their cars' cockpits, proved simply unbeatable.

In Britain, the British Racing Drivers' Club organised its British Empire Trophy road race on part of the motor-cycle TT course plus a round-the-houses section at Douglas, Isle of Man. The ex-Brooklands Junior Car Club, soon to become the British Automobile Racing Club, initiated a new International Road Race in St Helier, on Jersey in the Channel Islands. The *Grand Prix de l'ACF* was also revived upon a characterless arterial-road circuit in the Parilly suburb of Lyons.

Whenever and wherever Alfa Corse ran, they won. Only when they did not enter a race did the rival Maseratis and ERAs, or the Talbot-Lagos and Delahayes, stand any realistic chance.

Maserati's 4-cylinder supercharged *Vetturetti* won at Pau (Pagani), Jersey (Parnell), Nîmes, Nice, Strasbourg and Lausanne (all Villoresi) and Reims (Christian Kautz). The big rumbling Talbot-Lagos took first place at Perpignan and Marseille (both Eugéne Chaboud), Albi (Louis Rosier), Comminges (Louis Chiron) and Montlhéry (Yves Giraud-Cabantous). They also achieved the major success of the season, from a French perspective, when Louis Chiron drove Paul Vallée's *Écurie France* car to win the *Grand Prix de l'ACF* at Lyons-Parilly.

Alfa Corse concentrated, quite properly, on the great *Grande Épreuve* events which had pre-war counted towards the European Championship and which would subsequently – from 1950 – qualify for Drivers' and later Constructors' World Championship status. In the Swiss Grand Prix at Berne in June, Achille Varzi won Heat One, Wimille Heat Two and the Final. The French star added the Belgian Grand Prix trophy later that month, Varzi won the lesser Italian home fixture at Bari, and then Trossi took the Italian Grand Prix laurels in Alfa's Milanese backyard.

It was left to the well-prepared but otherwise uncompetitive British ERAs to pick up the crumbs – Bob Gerard's B-Type winning the Ulster Trophy at Ballyclare and the British Empire Trophy on the Isle of Man.

Then on October 23 1947, the doors of the *Grand Palais* in the Champs Élysées, Paris, opened on the second postwar *Salon de l'Automobile* exhibition. The accent there was on small, light and inexpensive cars to suit postwar pockets under austerity conditions. During the *Salon* the FIA's sporting commission met to review motor racing's future. They reached several important decisions.

Above all they confirmed that the existing *fait accompli* of 1.5-litre supercharged and 4.5-litre unsupercharged classes should apply for Grand Prix racing until the end of 1953, six more full seasons. However, from 1 January 1948 any type of fuel would be permitted in place of the alcohol-only restrictions applied perforce since the resumption of serious competition in 1946. In addition, the meeting agreed to adopt a new

THE CARS COMPETING – 1947

Alfa Romeo 158 and ex-*Bimotore* Alfa-Aitken; Grand Prix Alta; BMW 328/Frazer Nash*; Bugatti *Type* 35 and 51; The Challenger-Delage; Cisitalia D46; CTA-Arsenal; Darl'mat-Peugeot; Darracq; DB-Citroën *Spéciale*; Delage *Type Grand Prix* and D670; Delahaye 135; ERA A-Type, B-Type, C-Type, D-Type and E-Type; Frazer Nash-BMW 328*; Guérin; Lancia Astura Special; Maserati 4CL and 6CM; Riley Special; Simca-Gordini; Talbot-Lago *Monoplace*; *Type* 26C, T150C *Spéciale* and Lago SS Modifié; Testadoro *Spéciale*. (*German-built BMW 328 sports using the English Frazer Nash concessionaire's name to gain entry into a French race as anti-German feeling was still running high in France.)

Voiturette Formula for unsupercharged cars of no more than 2000cc capacity and supercharged cars of no more than 500cc.

To differentiate these two International single-seater Formulae, the Grand Prix class was referred to initially as Formula A, the *Voiturette* class as Formula B. To the public at large they would become better known, respectively, as Formula 1 and Formula 2.

8 May 1947 – JCC Jersey Road Race, St Helier, Channel Islands – Raymond Sommer practising his Maserati 4CL swings on to the seafront promenade at St Helier. Note the lobster-pot style oil cooler, the extensive body louvring, lock-wired undertray fixings, cord-bound steering-wheel rim, fuel tank breather pipe along the tail spine and the ventilated brake drum within that wire-spoked rear wheel; all so typical of the front-engined Grand Prix car around the war years.

Jersey Road Race, St Helier – Several of the better cars to have survived the war were restored and prepared in beautiful fettle to continue their racing careers. This is R.E. (Bob) Ansell's 1500 cc Maserati 4CL, seen in magnificent aesthetic order at the pits on St Helier promenade. Unfortunately, it didn't run in the race as well as it looked, its disgruntled owner retiring on the second lap with apparent piston failure. The 4CL's type number was derived from *4 cilindri linguetti* – "four cylinder 'tongues'", the anatomical reference being to the extended shape of the cam followers which actuated the unit's four valves per cylinder. A single Roots-type supercharger was used, drawing through a Weber carburettor. The chassis had independent front suspension by wishbones and torsion bars and a live rear axle on quarter-elliptic leafsprings. A four-speed gearbox in unit with the engine was operated by a cranked lever rising between the driver's legs.

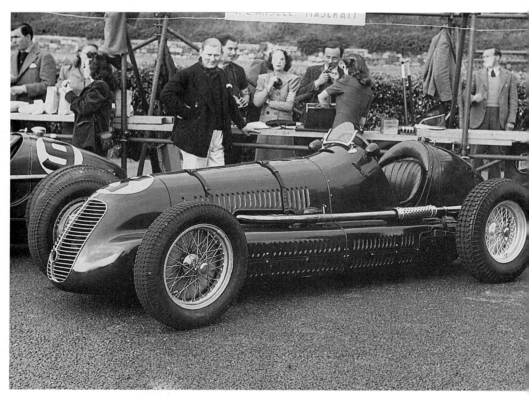

Jersey Road Race, St Helier – One of Louis Gérard's French *Écurie Gersac* Delage D670s, three of which were entered for Henri Louveau (number 25 seen here), the ill-fated 'Levegh' – Pierre Bouillon, the driver who would die at Le Mans in 1955 when his Mercedes-Benz 300SLR crashed opposite the pits – and Pierre Achard. Louveau finished fifth, 'Levegh' and Achard seventh and eighth. At the end of the race Gérard and Louis Chiron – on behalf of the *Scuderia Milano* Maserati team, both protested

the results concerning the relative positions of the leading cars. The RAC Stewards investigated fully, and ruled the timekeepers' original results valid. Delage had merged with one-time sports car racing rival Delahaye in 1935. Their D670 was a 2.7-litre whose short stroke made it more at home at high rpm than the better-known *Type* 135 Delahaye. A D670 finished fourth at Le Mans and Louis Gérard won the 1938 Donington TT in one rebodied in broadly Delahaye style. A more streamlined version was second at Le Mans. Six D670s were laid down in 1945 for the *Union Sportive Automobile* and, stripped of wings and lights, they competed widely in Formula events such as this.

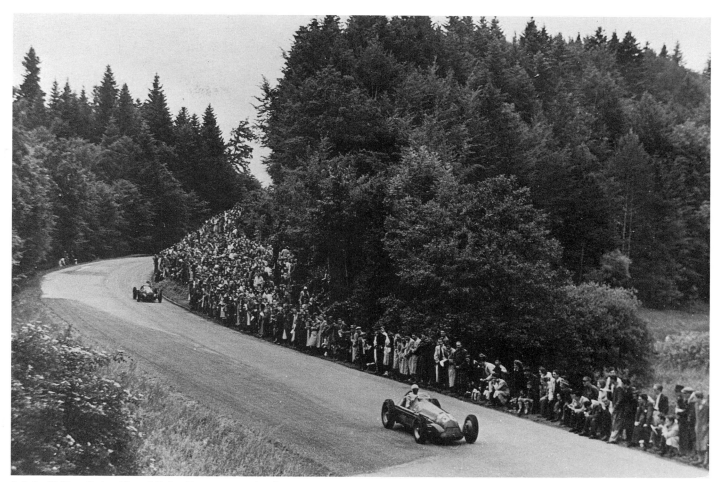

8 July 1947 – Swiss Grand Prix, Bremgarten circuit, Berne – *Alfettas* dominated again, here Varzi leads Trossi, first and second in Heat One, but both humbled by Wimille to finish behind him, second and third in the Final. Now look at the spectators, lining the roadside, totally unprotected yet craning forward. Reputedly there were no footbridges. Many spectators risked crossing the track to obtain a better view. On Varzi's slowing down lap after winning this Heat, his *Alfetta* struck and fatally injured a small boy dashing across the road. Amazingly for Switzerland, the crowds persistently ignored police instructions to assume safer positions, and in Heat Two two more died when Leslie Johnson's 4-litre sports Darracq locked a rear brake and merely ran a wheel a foot or so over the grass verge on which they stood, having just refused police advice to move. The Final started 90 minutes late after lorry loads of police arrived to assert control. The crowd still flooded the course when Wimille won and he refused to do a *tour d'honneur*. It was a sad postwar revival for what had pre-war been one of the greatest of all Grands Prix on this very fast and dauntingly tree-lined circuit.

Overleaf: Swiss Grand Prix, Berne – The things they'd do. Sommer's *Scuderia Milano*-entered Maserati 4CL again, here in practice. It was a warm sunny day and it seems they'd had cooling trouble – see the radiator draught includers? For the race itself these includers were excluded. Larger holes were cut in the 'cheeks' each side, flanking the grille, and slots appeared in the top of the nose. Their presence meant replacing the single nose-top race number 22 with numerals each side of the bonnet. When race day proved bright but cooler, with a threat of showery rain, the radiator grille had to be part blanked in any case. Note the crude supplementary oil tank ousting the usual external oil cooler and provided with a tap and feed pipe to the main under-seat oil supply. In the final Sommer still split the *Alfettas* away from the start. He finished fourth, ahead of Alfa test driver Sanesi's 158. What is more his fastest lap from Heat Two remained unbeaten by all the works *Alfettas*.

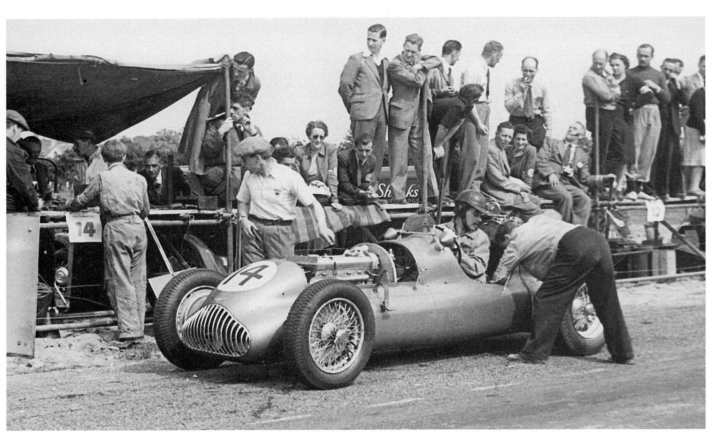

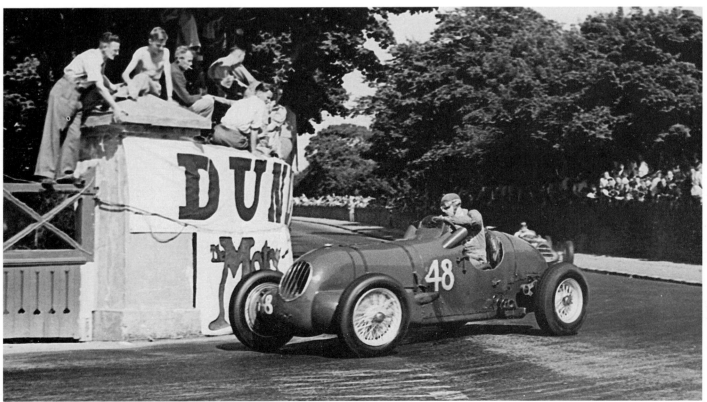

Left: 9 August 1947 – Ulster Trophy, Ballyclare – Gordon Watson in the pits with the Grand Prix Alta which he shared with wartime fighter pilot Bob Cowell, later to become famous as one of the first trans-sexuals to re-emerge as Roberta after a "Bob's your Auntie" operation. He and Watson had been in partnership as Cowell-Watson and were involved in promoting several ambitious plans for postwar British racing teams and projects, including the Aspin rotary-valve engine. They also ran the Leacroft of Egham coachworks which built many competition car bodies, including those for the HW-Alta and HWM series. The Grand Prix Alta seen here was built by Geoffrey Taylor's tiny Tolworth company, and featured a 1½-litre supercharged 4-cylinder engine in a twin-tube chassis with all-independent wishbone suspension using hard rubber blocks as the springing medium. Three were built; the first for George Abecassis, this the second and the third for the Irishman, Joe Kelly. They were generally underpowered and overweight but Geoffrey Taylor remained the first British constructor to introduce a postwar Grand Prix car, and his 4-cylinder twin-overhead camshaft engines subsequently introduced HWM and later powered both Connaught and Cooper chassis. This particular race was disastrous, eight starters and just two finishers, Bob Gerard's ERA and Barry Woodall's 1927 straight-eight Delage. Watson crashed through the hedge at Sandy Mount on lap 14, mangling the Alta's wheels but escaping without injury.

Below left: 21 August 1947 – British Empire Trophy race, Douglas, Isle of Man – Major A.P.R. (Tony) Rolt muscles his ex-Peter Aitken Alfa-Aitken Special into Parkfield Corner on the 6.25 km (3.88 ml) Manx motor racing circuit. His machine had started life in 1935 as one of the two Scuderia Ferrari-built Alfa Romeo *Bimotore* cars with one *Tipo B Monoposto* straight-eight supercharged engine in the nose and another in the tail, both driving the rear wheels. Austin Dobson had brought this car to Brooklands in 1937 but after some abortive outings there and at Donington Park he sold it to the Hon Peter Aitken who had it effectively cut in two, removing the rear engine, transmission and suspension. A new back axle was mounted on quarter-elliptic springs and an ENV pre-selector gearbox mated to the forward engine. This *Monomotore* was then rebodied and raced briefly as the Alfa-Aitken in 1939 until the outbreak of the war in which Aitken died. Postwar the car was acquired by R.V. Wallington who won with it in Britain's first postwar race meeting, at Gransden Lodge aerodrome in 1946. He then sold it to Tony Rolt, wartime inmate of Colditz Castle and one of the PoWs behind the celebrated "glider escape" attempt there. Freddie Dixon of pre-war Riley fame prepared the car, removing its twin superchargers, fitting eight SU carburettors and enlarging the engine to 3.4-litres to compete in Formula 1 under the unsupercharged 4½-litre allowance. Here its oil pressure zeroed after running fifth, far behind the supercharged 1½-litre Maseratis and ERAs. The following year Rolt would place second in the inaugural Dutch Grand Prix at Zandvoort.

Below: British Empire Trophy, Douglas – Reg Parnell's self-built Grand Prix car, the Challenger, started life in 1939 at a time when it seemed certain that the new Grand Prix Formula, due in 1941, would demand supercharged 1½-litre cars. His chassis was finished and fitted with an ERA engine and gearbox in time to run once at Prescott hill-climb before war broke out. It used a twin-tube frame with coil and wishbone independent front suspension while its de Dion rear suspension had torsion bar springs – all very 'Mercedes-Benz'. Parnell planned to fit a twin-overhead camshaft 6-cylinder engine derived from the MG Magnette unit of which he had considerable experience. Initially the car was christened 'The Challenge', but this evolved into 'Challenger'

as the war engulfed whatever chance it had. Postwar, Parnell revived the car with a 1927 Delage straight-eight engine from the enormous pile of parts he had acquired from Prince Chula. David Hampshire is driving the car here, but he retired with magneto trouble after 21 laps – the car showing no sign of competitiveness.

Left: 21 September 1947 – *Grand Prix de l'ACF*, Lyons-Parilly – Reg Parnell's second British hope of Grand Prix success was one of the two ill-starred E-Type ERAs, in this case chassis 'GP1'. ERA had begun design of a 3-litre Grand Prix contender for the 1938-40 3-litres supercharged/4½-litres unsupercharged Formula and even progressed to a running, 'stretched' 2-litre prototype but budgetary reality persuaded company backer Humphrey Cook he could not sustain the ambition of his partners, Raymond Mays and Peter Berthon. Consequently the E-Type emerged as a supercharged 1½-litre *voiturette*, but it showed little form before war broke out. In 1946 'GP1' was sold to Peter Whitehead, a sister 'GP2' being completed for Leslie Brooke. Whitehead sold 'GP1' to Reg Parnell after its failure in the 1947 Jersey Road Race, while Brooke ambitiously shipped 'GP2' to the Indianapolis 500-Miles, but gearbox trouble prevented him even trying to qualify. Both E-Types ran in the Marne Grand Prix at Reims, Brooke stopping after one lap with further gearbox trouble and Parnell retiring soon after, having started unsupercharged as his Zoller blower had disintegrated in practice. Starting money was the key! Running Jamieson-Roots two-stage supercharging in the Ulster Trophy, Parnell inherited the lead only for the de Dion tube to break. At Douglas, Brooke's 'GP2' finished, but here the following month it started minus a rod and piston, again just to earn its start money. Parnell's 'GP1' was lying tenth in this shot at the 1947 *Grand Prix de l'ACF* when Reg (complaining of poor handling) handed over to his chief mechanic, 'Wilkie' Wilkinson, who subsequently had a fright when a steering column pin sheared. Fortunately he came to a safe halt.

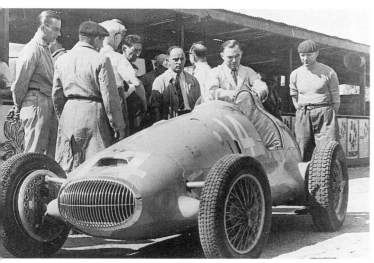
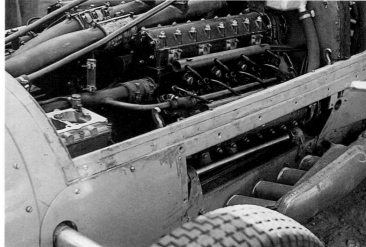

Grand Prix de l'ACF, Lyons-Parilly – Designer Albert Lory had made his racing reputation with the wonderful 1½-litre straight-eight Grand Prix Delages of 1926-7. Ten years later he was involved in the design of revised new independent front suspension chassis for these cars as then acquired by Prince Chula. Postwar he led design of the new French national racing car, the CTA-Arsenal. It was intended to retrieve *La Gloire* lost in Grand Prix racing. The French had already made a decidedly unsuccessful try at such a project in 1935 with the geared-crankshaft parallel-8 engined SEFAC – a truly hopeless flop. Now the *Centre d'Études Techniques de l'Automobile et du Cycle* was a Government-backed body, cost was no object and the work was undertaken at the State Arsenal – hence CTA-Arsenal.

Lory designed a two-stage supercharged 1½-litre four-camshaft V8 for which 266 bhp was claimed at 7500 rpm. A neat all-independent chassis featured coil-springs and sliders in the hub carriers like the pre-war Alta. It was quite pretty, but upon the first car's début here at Lyons, driver Raymond Sommer engaged the clutch at the start and a half-shaft snapped. Two CTAs practiced for the 1948 Grand Prix at Reims, but were finally withdrawn before the race. No attempt was made to race them again. Look at those sad faces – and see how the exhaust passed through the main chassis side members.

Above: Grand Prix de l'ACF, Lyons-Parilly – the veteran Louis Chiron's victorious Talbot-Lago, according subsequently to its driver, had a blowing head seal for much of the 511 km (317 ml) race, and although its engine fired generally on all six cylinders, it also spat and banged under hard acceleration. Consequently Chiron nursed it most of the way. It was Talbot's 1939 prototype *monoplace centrale* which had been accompanied that season by two sports-derived offset-seat, or *monoplace décalée,* cars. Raymond Mays had given this one its début in the 1939 Grand Prix at Reims-Gueux. Postwar it was acquired by Paul Vallée for his *Écurie France* team, driven variously by Sommer and Chiron. This was its greatest victory.

Opposite top: Grand Prix de l'ACF, Lyons-Parilly – When is a sports car not a sports car? French enthusiasts worked desperately hard to arm themselves with open-wheeler Grand Prix cars just postwar. This lofty but rather attractive device is Maurice Varet's Delahaye 135-based Grand Prix *Traction Avant* special, the engine being reversed to couple with (possibly) Citroën transmission to drive the front wheels. It was slow but reliable, finishing 9th, too far behind to be classified a finisher. It used the 3.6-litre 6-cylinder engine and had most unusual fabricated sheet spoke wheels. Much time and thought had evidently been invested in this not very successful but nonetheless rare and very interesting private-owner's Grand Prix car.

Right: Grand Prix de l'ACF, Lyons-Parilly – Another 'single-seaterized' sports car, in this case Louis Rosier's Talbot-Lago *Modifiée,* we believe being driven in practice here by reserve driver Morel. Ex-Fiat designer Walter Becchia was Lago's long-serving Chief Engineer who created the new *Type* 150C sports car chassis and 4-litre hemi-headed engine in 1935. He saved weight and improved manouevrability by shortening the existing chassis' wheelbase, and in the winter of 1936-7 Talbot company owner Anthony Lago authorized development of the 'Lago SS' high-performance lightweight model using this T150C frame. The English took the initials to mean Special Short. Some wonderfully rakish and extravagant bodies were then fitted; most notably by Figoni et Falaschi. For early postwar racing Eugène Chaboud converted one Lago SS into a wide whale-like *biplace course,* and Louis Rosier – the haulier and *garagiste* from Clermont-Ferrand – built this sleeker, similarly offset-seat, version from a Figoni et Falaschi Cabriolet. Here he finished fourth.

34

1948

THE NEW FORMULAE BEGIN...

Among 18 of the new Formula 1 races run in Europe in 1948, nine fell to Maserati, two each to ERA and Talbot-Lago, the only four that mattered to Alfa Romeo and one, a significant first, to Enzo Ferrari's new marque from Maranello.

Maserati made the most significant advance of the season in introducing their twin-tubular chassis *Tipo* 4CLT/48 cars with two-stage supercharged 16-valve 4-cylinder engine. These cars developed some 240bhp and weighed around 1,350lbs against the straight-eight *Alfetta*'s 350bhp and similar weight. These attractive new Maseratis could not match the débutante supercharged V12 Ferrari *Tipo* 125 nor the Alfa Romeo 158s for either power or sheer speed, but they handled infinitely better than the former and tolerably close to the latter, and were both available and affordable to an established and enthusiastic private clientéle. In addition, Maserati retained the services of two very fine drivers in the experienced Luigi Villoresi and his brilliant if burly young protegé, Alberto Ascari – son of the 1924-5 Alfa Romeo star driver, Antonio.

In Paris, Major Antoine Lago's *Automobiles Talbot* factory was by this time in series production with its own variation upon the Grand Prix car theme. Their *Type* 26 *Course Monoplace* or *26C* also found customers from a number of enthusiastic, predominantly French, private owner-drivers.

In England, Geoffrey Taylor's tiny Alta Engineering Company had struggled to launch a viable Grand Prix car design on to the owner-driver market as early as 1945. He had little success, as most prospective owner-drivers saw Italian Maseratis or Old English Upright pre-war ERAs as far more reliable and raceworthy propositions. Most vitally, they felt they could command better start and bonus money payments from race organisers if they were entering a proven car – like a Maserati.

Rodney Walkerley, Sports Editor of *The Motor*, wrote of 1948: "It was evident that there were as many potential Grand Prix drivers in Britain as there had been before the war but now, as then, they had no cars comparable with the foreign opposition . . .".

Raymond Mays, father of ERA, had long-since founded his remarkable V16-cylinder 1.5-litre BRM co-operative project, but its progress had been pitifully slow and troubled and the car would not emerge for nearly two more years.

On March 23 1948, this new era of Formula 1 racing was launched at Pau. Racing motorcyclist Nello Pagani won this minor French round-the-houses Grand Prix for the second successive year, Maserati-mounted, of course.

In May, Dr Farina won both the *Grand Prix des Nations* and the revived Monaco Grand Prix in his Maserati 4CL and then on June 27 two of Maserati's brand-new 4CLTs made their début in the San Remo Grand Prix on the coastal Ospedaletti circuit and finished first and second, Ascari leading home Villoresi. The *San Remo* Maserati had been born.

In July the Swiss Grand Prix also carried the courtesy title *Grand Prix d'Europe*. Alfa Romeo entered but Ferrari, though much-discussed, were still not ready with their new *monoposto*. Final practice was marred by rain. Farina's 4CLT set fastest time until Wimille went out for Alfa Romeo, hacking a whole 12.4 secs off the Italian's best. Achille Varzi, ever-resentful of the French star's presence in this most Italian of teams, was unable to approach either time. He insisted upon taking out the team's experimental two-stage supercharged car, but lost control and crashed. It was a freakish, low-speed accident, in which the car spun before running quite slowly tail-first up a bank. It then toppled over. Poor Varzi was half ejected from the cockpit and trapped by his head between the windscreen and the ground. The ice-man, who had earlier suffered only one serious racing accident, was dead.

Next day, on the opening lap of the race, Christian Kautz, the Swiss driver who had driven for both Mercedes-Benz and Auto Union pre-war, crashed his Maserati fatally. Berne's Bremgarten circuit was never one to take prisoners . . .

Wimille, under team orders, demonstrated his superiority by motoring off into a comfortable lead before making a leisurely pit-stop to add unwanted water. Once Trossi had gone by to assume the lead, Wimille rejoined to trail him home a dutiful second. Sanesi placed fourth in the other *Alfetta*.

At Reims for the *Grand Prix de l'ACF* it was the Frenchman's turn to win, Ascari finishing third in his only Grand Prix for Alfa Corse, behind Sanesi. Despite making the usual two refuelling stops each, these *Alfettas* finished some nine miles ahead of the three surviving Talbot-Lagos which completed the 310 miles non-stop. This was a true measure of the mismatch between contemporary supercharged 1½-litre cars and the big unblown 4½s.

The Italian Grand Prix was held that year in Turin's Valentino Park, over just 224 miles in torrential rain. Ferrari's new V12s at last emerged, three to be driven by Farina, Raymond Sommer and 'B.Bira'. In these three drivers one can perceive something of the approach which Enzo Ferrari always applied: a top-line professional racing driver at the head; talented but above all wealthy and patrician potential customer-drivers in support.

Wimille boomed round the flooded circuit looking wet and bored at an uncatchable pace for Alfa Corse with Villoresi's Maserati and Sommer's Ferrari 125 in hopeless, and virtually brakeless, pursuit.

October 1948 saw the inaugural postwar British Grand Prix run on one of the new-fangled temporary race circuits using wartime aerodrome tracks. This was the best the British could manage in view of laws preventing the closure of public roads for racing. The aerodrome in question was Silverstone, in Northamptonshire.

Neither Alfa Corse nor the new Ferrari marque could be persuaded to attend, while Ascari and Villoresi in their quasi-works Maserati 4CLT/48s both arrived too late to practice. They consequently started from the back of the grid behind a motley assortment of other Maseratis, elderly ERAs and hefty Talbots. Yet just nine miles into the race, the two 4CLT/48s were firmly established ahead of this field and after their two scheduled refuelling stops they finished first and second, Luigi Villoresi some 14 secs ahead of his young friend after a 250-mile demonstration.

At the re-opened Monza circuit in the *Gran Premio dell'Autodromo*, Alfa Corse again demonstrated their peerless class with J-P Wimille, inevitably, winning as he pleased. According to Consalvo Sanesi, who set fastest lap in this race, it was he who had been scripted to win, but against team orders Count Trossi rushed ahead near the end as the chief tester's own car began to falter. On seeing Trossi's move, Wimille decided the Italian should be put in his place and, with a sympathetic wave to Sanesi as he too tore by, the Frenchman outdrove Trossi – and stole another win.

Into that winter, the Alfa Romeo board announced that Alfa Corse was to withdraw from racing in 1949 owing to financial strictures, the company being state-owned and the Government having ordered economies.

But on October 24, 1948, the Italian season had ended in the *Circuito di Garda* race, which Dr Farina won comfortably in the short-chassis, tricky to handle but undeniably powerful new Ferrari 125. This was the first-ever success for a *monoposto* racing car carrying Enzo Ferrari's own name. It was to be the first of many.

THE CARS COMPETING – 1948

Alfa Romeo 158, *Tipo B monoposto* and ex-*Bimotore* Alfa-Aitken; Grand Prix Alta; BMW 328; Bugatti *Type* 51A Special (CDL) and 59; Cisitalia D46; CTA-Arsenal; Darl'mat-Peugeot; DB-Panhard; Delage D670 and *Type Grand Prix*; Delahaye 135; Emeryson-Duesenberg; ERA B-Type, C-Type, D-Type and E-Type; Ferrari 125 and 166; Jicey; Lagonda; Maserati 4CLT/48, 4CL and 6CM; RRA-ERA; Riley Special; SEFAC; Simca-Gordini; Talbot-Lago *Monoplace 1939*, T26C, T150C and Lago SS *modifié*; Todd *Spéciale*; Veritas Meteor.

25 May 1948 – British Empire Trophy Race, Douglas, Isle of Man – Abecassis in the first purpose-built postwar British Grand Prix car, the Geoffrey Taylor-designed and made Grand Prix Alta. A sister car to the Gordon Watson and Joe Kelly (two-stage) supercharged machines it featured similar all-independent wishbone suspension by rubber block, and was quite a handsome beast but too heavy for its relatively modest power. Chassis number was 'GP1'. The slot in the bonnet does not denote anything so technical as a supercharger relief valve vent, as on a Bugatti; it was merely a hand hold for the bonnet to be removed and replaced. Beautifully built shell though, wasn't it?

18 July 1948 – *Coupe des Petites Cylindrées*, Reims-Gueux – Not a Grand Prix Formula race, but just look at the emergent names on the grid of this *Voiturette* event; names and numbers are Sommer (Ferrari 166 26) who won; Fangio (Simca-Gordini 6), 'Bira' (Simca-Gordini 2), Flahaut (Simca-Gordini 4), Prince Igor Troubetskoy (Ferrari 166 42), each of whom retired; Manzon (Simca-Gordini 10, seventh), 'Nando Righetti (Ferrari 166 28, second); Roger Loyer (Veritas, 22, rtd) and Ciro Basadonna (Cisitalia D46, 50, rtd).

Coupe des Petites Cylindrées, Reims-Gueux – Ciro Basadonna's kiddy car-like Fiat 1100-engined Dante Giacosa-designed Cisitalia D46 displaying its lines beside the dog house in the Reims paddock; it employed the first multi-tubular spaceframe chassis to be used in a series-production racing car. Note its comfy chair for the man and almost motor-cycle sized front tyres. At this time in the UK a different poor man's racing formula was just finding its feet, for 500cc motor-cycle engined cars; but their engines were mainly in the rear to clear a chain-drive run to the back wheels.

18 July 1948 – *Grand Prix de l'ACF*, Reims-Gueux – Juan Manuel Fangio, the Argentine visitor, driving in his first *Grande Épreuve* at the wheel of the works Simca-Gordini T15 – chassis 08 GC – in which he had previously retired that weekend from the *Coupe des Petites Cylindrées*. Fangio had first been given a 1220 cc Simca-Gordini drive in Rosario, Argentina, during the *Temporada* race series on February 1, leading number one driver Wimille who reported "Given a first-class car, Fangio would do great things!". The Argentine drove the Gordini again in the Palermo Park, Buenos Aires, race two weeks later, finishing eighth. Further encouraged by Achille Varzi, Fangio joined a fact-finding trip to Europe by the *Automovil Club Argentino* – the ACA. They saw the San Remo Grand Prix on June 27, where the latest Maserati 4CLT/48s won first time out, and ultimately decided to buy a pair for their own 1949 team in Europe. Varzi was then killed in practice for the Swiss Grand Prix in which Gordini driver Maurice Trintignant was gravely injured. Two weeks later, at Amedée Gordini's invitation, Fangio replaced him here at Reims. He lost some 11 minutes with an ignition problem before the fuel tank finally split, losing a distant twelfth place.

Left: Coupe des Petites Cylindrées, Reims-Gueux – 'Nando Righetti finished second for the new name on the circuits, a name which was on everybody's lips as it progressed towards introducing true Grand Prix cars that autumn. The name was *Ferrari*. Here Righetti is power sliding his little 2-litre unsupercharged V12-engined Tipo 166 through the ninety-right in the centre of Gueux village, the corner which would be by-passed in later years by a very fast and deceptive right-hand curve constructed across farmland just short of the village outskirts. Ferrari's first customers for the 166 had been the Besana brothers, and in the *Grand Prix de l'ACF* itself Count Soave Besana drove his car, only to retire after 19 laps with engine trouble. These Ferraris could compete as sports cars with lights and cycle-type mudguards attached, or stripped (as here) in Formula 1 and Formula 2.

Left inset: 15 May 1948 – Monaco Grand Prix practice, Monte Carlo – Prince Igor Troubetskoy, White Russian and sometime husband of Barbara Hutton the Woolworth heiress, bought one of the very earliest Ferrari 166 sports-cum-Formula cars which is here being readied for the owner. Note the new Italian car's very compact build, front suspension detail, the starting handle protruding from the grille and the race number form which appears to have been yellow outlined in black or very dark blue – which could look lovely on a scale model Ferrari. Much was made in the contemporary press about Ferrari's "twelve cylinders and five speeds". 'Prince Igor' as he was listed in entries of the time, was a capable driver, who went quite well in the Grand Prix before skidding into the barriers at the chicane after 58 laps, damaging this car too badly to continue.

Main picture: Grand Prix de l'ACF, Reims-Gueux – The unique occasion on which Alberto Ascari raced an Alfa Corse *Alfetta*, braking hard into Gueux Corner on his way to finishing third behind his temporary team-mates, Wimille and Sanesi. Alberto's Champion father – Antonio Ascari – had won the 1924 French, Belgian and Italian Grands Prix in his works Alfa Romeo P2s before losing his life in one while leading the *Grand Prix de l'ACF* at Montlhéry in 1925. Signor Gallo, President of Alfa Romeo, had driven from Milan to see this 1948 version and his team arrived with "eight or nine open and closed five-ton trucks, and two spare racing cars, one being a 158A and the other a 158, to be kept behind the pits in case any spares were needed during the course of the race. There was also a mobile workshop equipped with a welding plant, benches and vices, and an independent petrol engine and dynamo supplying the power to drive a lathe and drilling machine . . .". Alfa Corse raced to win. Wimille did just that, as usual, while Ascari was third to team orders within a half-second of Sanesi. Henceforth, Ascari would only drive Grand Prix cars for Maserati, Ferrari and ultimately Lancia.

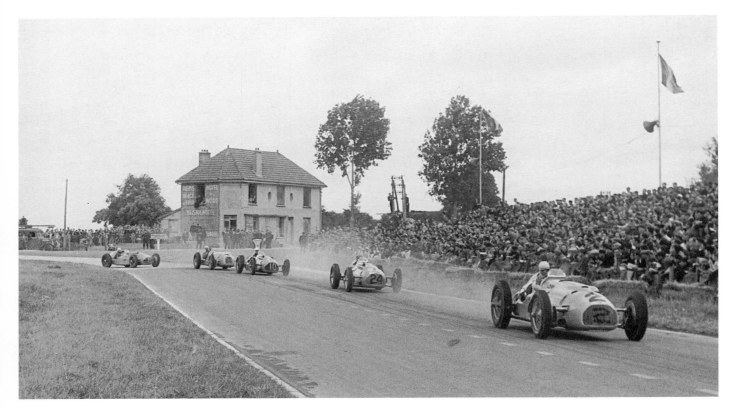

Grand Prix de l'ACF, Reims-Gueux – Local pursuit of the Alfa Romeos made a brave sight, the stomach-rumbling 4½-litre Talbot-Lagos accelerating away from Thillois Corner towards the tribunes being led here by Louis Chiron (*Monoplace Central '39* number 2, ninth on the road but too far behind to be classified), followed by Philippe Étancelin (T26C No 24, retired, 24 laps, engine), Gianfranco Comotti (T26C No 10, fourth behind the three *Alfettas*), Yves Giraud-Cabantous (*1939 Monoplace Décalée* No 4, retired, 31 laps, split fuel tank) and 'Raph' (T26C No 6, finished fifth).

5 September 1948 – Italian Grand Prix, Valentino Park, Turin – Villoresi's latest style 2-stage supercharged, twin-tube chassis Maserati 4CLT/48 entered by the quasi-works *Scuderia Ambrosiana* plumes around the city park accompanied by the new Formula 1 Ferrari 125, one of the three entered and driven here by Raymond Sommer. These 1½-litre single-stage supercharged Ferrari 125s combined relatively high power with an unusually short wheelbase, swing-axle rear suspension and, by contemporary standards, very light weight. They proved exceptionally nervous handlers in such atrocious conditions. These three new Ferrari *monoposti* were driven by Sommer, Farina and 'Bira'; and while Wimille won (of course) for Alfa Romeo with Villoresi comfortably second, Sommer was a courageous third and 'Bira's' transmission failed, while Farina slithered off into the straw bales.

2 October 1948 – RAC British Grand Prix, Silverstone – 'B.Bira' demonstrates the beautiful lines of the latest Formula 1 Maserati, the 4CLT/48, navigating his way around the wide open spaces of the marker-drum lined Silverstone airfield circuit. He finished fifth here in a race dominated by *Scuderia Ambrosiana's* quasi-works sister cars driven by Luigi Villoresi and Alberto Ascari which finished first and second.

1949
FERRARI SHINE IN ALFA'S ABSENCE

The postwar recovery rather faltered this year due in part to the continuing postwar recession but also due to race promoters' faltering confidence following Alfa Corse's withdrawal. The relevant authorities in Monaco and Spain both cancelled plans to run Grands Prix, while an energetic German attempt to revive a major-Formula event foundered in face of continuing French emnity.

In Alfa Corse's absence, Ferrari achieved major success with their single-camshaft V12-engined 125s, driven by the fine former Maserati pairing of Ascari and Villoresi. At Monza that September, the Italian Grand Prix returned to its spiritual home. There Ferrari introduced a two-stage supercharged V12 125 with twin overhead camshafts. These engines were also mounted in longer-wheelbase chassis offering very much more stable handling.

Tragedy had marred the season's opening in far-away Argentina as Jean-Pierre Wimille, the acknowledged master driver of the day, crashed fatally in a little Simca-Gordini while practising in Buenos Aires' Palermo Park.

Perhaps the most significant feature of this 1949 Formula 1 season was the sensational series of minor race wins recorded by the Argentine visitor to Europe, Juan Manuel Fangio. He and his travelling companion, Benedicto Campos, were sponsored by the national *Automovil Club Argentino* and the Argentine State-backed YPF oil company and were under the personal patronage of President Juan Peron himself. They had been tutored during the 1948 Argentine *Temporada* series by the late Achille Varzi and their path into European racing was smoothed by the dead Champion's father, who set at the

Argentine team's disposal his villa and the attached workshops in Galliate.

Using the Varzi villa as their home base, the ACA team tackled a full season of "manageable" Formula 1 races; the remarkable Fangio's blue-and-yellow 4CLT winning at San Remo, Pau, Perpignan and Albi.

Ferrari, meanwhile, began selling *Tipo* 125 Grand Prix cars to wealthy and influential privateers. Former ERA campaigner, Peter Whitehead, bought one of the earliest ultra-short wheelbase models while Enzo Ferrari supplied another on acceptable terms to Tony Vandervell whose British company supplied the *ThinWall* shell crankshaft bearings which did so much to make the Italian V12 a winner after initial difficulties. Vandervell was one of the captains of British industry who backed Raymond Mays' cooperative BRM project, but after four long years the proposed V16-cylinder Grand Prix car seemed as far away as ever from actually racing. Never a patient man, Vandervell had grown fidgety. Now he was determined for the BRM *équipe* to gain some first hand experience of what Grand Prix racing was all about.

At great expense his new green-painted Ferrari was to run in the British Grand Prix at Silverstone, driven by Mays himself with BRM chief mechanic Ken Richardson as second driver. The event attracted a field of meagre quality. Villoresi ran a Maserati in the absence of works Ferraris, and he faced the Vandervell car plus a fleet of other Maseratis, Talbot-Lagos and the inevitable old ERAs.

Villoresi led until the first fuel stop, then ran a bearing. Further down the field Ken Richardson took over the green Ferrari from an unhappy, and slow, Raymond Mays and spun into the crowd. The event ran out with the Swiss Baron Emmanuel 'Toulo' de Graffenried victorious in his Enrico Platé-prepared and entered Maserati 4CLT, from the reliable Bob Gerard flatteringly second in his beautifully-prepared ERA.

The sturdy and steady French Talbot-Lago owner-driver Louis Rosier finished third there, a month later winning the Belgian Grand Prix at Spa! Ascari and Villoresi drove their fast but still unpredictably-handling swing-axle works Ferraris, and Whitehead his older private example, but Rosier brilliantly exploited the long-range fuel capacity of his Talbot-Lago. This car was also at home on the Ardennes circuit's very fast, open curves, where the accent was upon continuous steady speed. After all their inevitable refuelling stops, Rosier was able to beat the Ferraris by some 49 secs.

The Swiss Grand Prix at Berne saw Ascari and Villoresi score Ferrari's first notable 1-2 finish, and for the *Grand Prix de France* at Reims-Gueux the European mainstream racers met the visiting Argentinian team for the first time at *Grande Épreuve* level. Villoresi, Fangio, Campos and 'Bira' duelled in the opening stages, the Argentines seizing the advantage after Villoresi encountered brake trouble. However, both ACA Maseratis eventually failed and 'Bira's Platé 4CLT emerged in the lead from Chiron's rapid Écurie France Talbot-Lago and Whitehead's privately-entered Ferrari.

Chiron inherited the lead as the Italian 1½-litre cars stopped to refuel. Whitehead rejoined in second place. After lapping at 105 mph he closed on the blue Talbot. Whitehead found a way by and after a brief duel began to draw clear. With the finish virtually in sight, the Englishman seemed set to win for Ferrari. Then the drain-plug loosened and fell out of his gearbox which promptly overheated and jammed in top gear. He could not hold on. He was repassed first by Chiron, who won again for France, and was further demoted to third place by 'Bira'. Chiron's victorious three-hour non-stop run averaged fractionally less than 100 mph. The previous season had seen Alfa Romeo win at 102.

At Zandvoort in the Dutch Grand Prix the three regular Ferraris again took on the Maseratis, excepting Fangio and Campos, and the Talbots. Farina and Reg Parnell were both penalized a minute for jumping the start, enabling Villoresi of Ferrari to set his pace by their's, winning easily by half a minute.

At Monza for the Italian GP, Ferrari introduced their latest long-wheelbase, 4-camshaft, de Dion rear axled *Tipo 125* cars for Ascari and Villoresi while Maserati's novelty was the Speluzzi-headed special from Scuderia Milano. Ascari proved unstoppable, finishing miles ahead of the veteran Frenchman Philippe Étancelin's Talbot and 'Bira's' even more tardy Maserati.

The Czechoslovakian Grand Prix was run again on the narrow but still magnificent Masarykring outside Brno, Farina and Parnell both crashing their Maseratis on the opening lap while 'Bira' joined them in the ditch on lap two. Trintignant's Simca-Gordini also succumbed, but Whitehead's cool and controlled style paid off brilliantly as he became the first British driver to win a premier-Formula race in Europe since Dick Seaman had succeeded in the German Grand Prix of 1938.

That December saw fresh hope for a British re-emergence on the International motor racing scene. The prototype BRM Type 15 V16 was unveiled on the bitterly cold and bleak wartime aerodrome at Folkingham, in Lincolnshire. It was received ecstatically by the national press – but significantly far more cautiously and sceptically by the specialist motoring journals.

They understood that motor racing is a difficult and demanding business. Many in the know doubted that BRM's organization was man enough for the task ahead.

THE COMPETING CARS – 1949

AFM; AJB; Alfa Romeo ex-*Bimotore* Alfa-Aitken; Grand Prix Alta; BMW 328; Bugatti *Type* 51A Special (CDL) and 59; Cooper-JAP 1000cc; Delage *Type Grand Prix*; Delahaye 135; ERA A-Type, B-Type, C-Type, D-Type and E-Type; Darracq; Ferrari 125 and 166; FN; HW-Alta; Jicey; Magda; Maserati 4CLT, 4CL, 6CM and A6; Meteor; RRA; Simca-Gordini; SVA; Talbot-Lago T26C; Tatraplan.

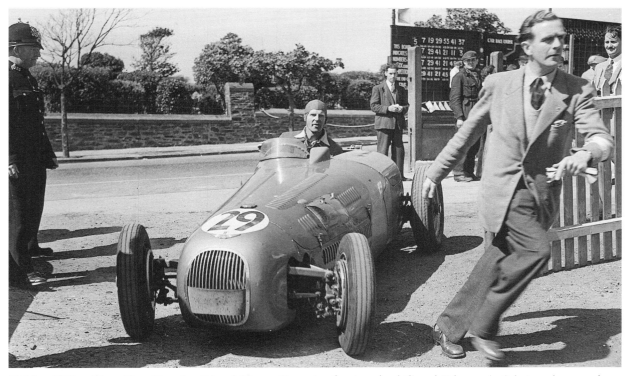

26 May 1949 – Manx Cup, Douglas, Isle of Man – No, not a front-engined Grand Prix car (yet) but an honoured forerunner of what would become a very successful if short-lived British marque – the HW-Alta driven here by its lofty constructor, John Heath, partner of George Abecassis in HW Motors Ltd at Walton-on-Thames. This little car was a dual-purpose Formula 2-cum-sports model based upon a Heath-designed, Walton-built twin-tube chassis with proprietary running gear and an Armstrong-Siddeley pre-selector gearbox. It was powered by an unblown Alta 2-litre 4-cylinder engine. Its successes in 1949 prompted Heath to field a team of four similar (apart from a significant change to independent rear suspension) cars under the HWM name in 1950 Formula 2, his pioneering team giving a great account of itself and giving such drivers as Stirling Moss, Lance Macklin and later Peter Collins their grounding in first class open-wheeler competition.

Left: 26 June 1949 – *Gran Premio dell'Autodromo*, Monza, Italy – Argentine visitor Juan Manuel Fangio in the new Ferrari which he has just run-in on the long public road drive from Maranello (!) in preparation for this Formula 2 race. The *Tipo* 166 used an unsupercharged 2-litre V12 engine and similarly short-wheelbase chassis/swing-axle rear suspension to the 125 Formula 1 version. Ferrari had refused to release the car to the ACA team until they paid and it took some frantic negotiation and intercontinental telephone calls by Fangio and team manager Pancho Borgonovo before an associate of President Perón, an enthusiastic ACA supporter named Alberto Dodero, cabled the necessary funds. Fangio collected the car from Maranello three days before the race. Despite being unable to find fifth gear, bubble-footing along the straights to avoid serious over-revving, Fangio profited by others' misfortune to win despite the engine being thoroughly cooked by the time he finished.

Above: 17 July 1949 – *Grand Prix de France*, Reims-Gueux – The mainstream *Grand Prix de l'ACF* that season being run for sports cars at Comminges due to internal French politics, the Reims race was styled the *Grand Prix de France* yet it catered for Formula 1 and in all but name it was 'the French Grand Prix'. Here is the man of the year, Fangio, in his blue-and-yellow ACA-owned Maserati 4CLT/48 – chassis '1514' – in which he won at San Remo, Pau, Perpignan and Albi but was forced to retire after leading here. He also drove the winning Simca-Gordini in the Marseilles Grand Prix, but retired the 4CLT from its other major full-length race, the Belgian Grand Prix at Spa. The father of the late Achille Varzi had put his son's home workshops in Galliate at the ACA team's disposal, and in tribute they ran as the Automovil Club Argentino's *Equipo Argentino Achille Varzi*.

Overleaf: 20 August 1949 – BRDC International Trophy, Silverstone – Alberto Ascari dominated this Formula 1 season's top level races in his works entered Ferrari 125s with their supercharged V12 engine. Here in England he was beaten by 'Bira's' 4CLT by 0.8 sec in Heat One before proving his clear superiority in the Final. This shot demonstrates the new Ferrari Grand Prix car's short wheelbase which helped minimise its weight – but which, when allied to considerable power and swing-axle rear suspension – endowed it with decidedly nervous handling. It demanded a driver of Ascari's exceptional quality to exploit its full potential.

25 September 1949 – Czechoslovakian Grand Prix, Masarykring, Brno – International racing having been revived on this famous pre-war venue, here at the start is the Scots accountant David Murray's Leslie Brooke-entered Maserati 4CLT/48 flanked by local opposition in the form of Bruno Sojka's works-developed rear-engined Tatraplan. While Murray was forced out after 11 laps with fuel starvation, Sojka finished ninth, best of the three Czech competitors as Vlcek's Magda and Dobry's FN were placed tenth and eleventh behind him. The race was most notable for Peter Whitehead's victory in his Ferrari, beating Étancelin's Talbot-Lago by 35.6 sec after 356 km (221 mls) of racing. Whitehead thus became the first English driver to win a premier-Formula Continental race since Dick Seaman's German Grand Prix victory for Mercedes in 1938.

1950

THE WORLD CHAMPIONSHIP BEGINS...

This new year saw the birth of the FIA's World Championship for Drivers, decided by results in a series of essentially Formula 1 *Grandes Épreuves*. However, the CSI also included the American Indianapolis 500-Miles speedway classic in the series. This expedient move was made largely to attract some trans-Atlantic interest in the series, interest which could have been repaid by Europe's star Grand Prix drivers seeking adequate rides in the classic American Memorial Day Sweepstake. It was, however, an illogical move in that Formula 1 was a road racing class while Indianapolis and United States Auto Club oval-track racing in general catered for highly specialised speedway cars using mainly four-cylinder unsupercharged 4.2-litre Offenhauser engines.

In reality, hardly any European manufacturers and precious few Formula 1 drivers, ever attempted to attack the highly-specialized challenge of Indianapolis. Even fewer Indy constructors, entrants or drivers showed any interest at all in the relatively minuscule financial attractions of Formula 1 road racing in Europe. No Indy driver therefore stood a chance in the FIA Drivers' World Championship and neither did any European manufacturer or driver realistically stand a chance in the Indianapolis 500. Essentially the twain would not meet again to repeat the pre-First and Second World War European treks to the United States until the mid-1960s.

Perhaps the greatest effect achieved by the new World Championship was its projection of Alfa Corse back into competition. The Portello board made Alfa's comeback after their bye-season in 1949 thanks to financial support from Pirelli and their major distributors. After a race-free year in which to pursue quiet but continuous development of the legendary *Tipo* 158 cars they returned with a reliable 350 bhp at 8500 rpm available to their drivers.

Team director GianBattista Guidotti had now replaced the lost aces, Wimille, Varzi and Trossi (who died of lung cancer during the summer of 1949) with the 'Three-Fs' team of Farina, Fangio and the veteran pre-war Maserati and Mercedes-Benz star, Luigi Fagioli – the old 'Abruzzi Robber'.

Ferrari had replaced *Capo Ingegnere* Gioachino Colombo – the arch-priest of multi-cylinder supercharged engines and the pre-war originator of the *Alfetta* itself – with *Ing* Aurelio Lampredi. He was very much a practical man. He had little use for the complicated, difficult to make and costly supercharged $1\frac{1}{2}$-litre V12 and directed Ferrari's attention instead towards the practicality, economy, relatively light weight and immense mid-range torque of an unsupercharged $4\frac{1}{2}$-litre unit. Ascari and Villoresi again spearheaded Ferrari's driver team.

Talbot's clients for the big 6-cylinder cars were offered an improved twin-plug per cylinder head to boost output to some 275 bhp but these heavy cars were by this time decidedly antiquated. The Maserati 4CLTs were also showing their age, the little 4-cylinder 16-valve supercharged engines on the limit of their development potential. They remained merely a private entrants' proposition, never a works team car. Simca-Gordini remained underpowered, often over-raced and unreliable – and French.

British hopes rested on the unproven V16-cylinder BRM which on paper should have destroyed both Alfa Romeo and Ferrari. Nevertheless, paper projects do not win races, and the BRM in the metal, and in the organisation of its team, amounted to considerably less than it had promised.

The British Grand Prix at Silverstone opened the new World Championship of Drivers on 13 May 1950. Alfa Corse dominated both the starting grid and the race with four *Alfetti* driven by Farina, Fangio, Fagioli and Britain's best-established driver invited for the weekend – Reg Parnell. Fangio struck a straw bale and retired

with a broken oil pipe to leave Farina, Fagioli and Parnell to roar deafeningly home 1-2-3 for Alfa Corse.

The Championship series was then completed by the Monaco Grand Prix, the Indianapolis 500, the Swiss, Belgian, French and Italian Grands Prix. Alfa Corse won every European round, in the sequence Fangio, Farina, Fangio, Fangio, Farina. The Italian's extra fourth place in the Belgian Grand Prix against Fangio's failure to score at Silverstone and Berne, made Farina motor racing's first official World Champion Driver.

At the end of that season, the final World Championship of Drivers table looked like this:

Farina, World Champion Driver, with 30 points
Fangio, 2nd, with 27 points
Fagioli, 3rd, with 24 points
Louis Rosier (Talbot-Lago), 4th, with 13 points
Alberto Ascari (Ferrari), 5th, with 11 points
'B.Bira' (Maserati), 6th, with 5 points

'Bira's' sixth place in my listing was officially only eighth, since the first and second place finishers at Indianapolis – Johnny Parsons and Bill Holland – by the CSI's reckoning secured nine and six Championship points respectively. Neither made any attempt at Formula 1 road racing and to all intents and purposes (other than historical perspective) they may be ignored here.

Of course the usual full season of more modest Formula 1 races took place, 1950 seeing no fewer than 15 non-Championship events. Alfa Corse contested only four of them; at Bari, Geneva, Pescara and in the International Trophy at Silverstone. Of course they won each time (Farina and Fangio taking two each). The Argentinian had also won at Pau in his ACA team Maserati 4CLT, while Parnell's similar car won the minor Richmond Trophy at Goodwood.

Talbot won three times, Georges Grignard taking the *Grand Prix de Paris* at Montlhéry and Rosier the Albi and Dutch Grands Prix, while Bob Gerard's faithful ERA won the parochial British Empire Trophy at Douglas, IoM. Ferrari's 125 in Peter Whitehead's hands took the Jersey Road Race and Ulster Trophy at Dundrod. The new unsupercharged Ferrari 375 then won at Barcelona in Ascari's skilled hands, and the brand-new BRM won a very short and flooded Goodwood race in the brave and rugged hands of Reg Parnell.

It had been a busy and successful season.

THE CARS COMPETING – 1950

AJB; Alfa Romeo 158; Alta Grand Prix; BRM Type 15; CDL; Cooper-JAP 1000 and 1100cc; Delage D670 and *Type Grand Prix*; ERA A-Type, B-Type, E-Type; Ferrari 125, 166, 275 and 375; HWM; Maserati 4CLT, 4CL and 6CM; Maserati-Milan; MG R-Type; RRA; Talbot-Lago T26C; Simca-Gordini.

Right: Swiss Grand Prix, Bremgarten – Ascari's team-mate Villoresi trying equally hard in the latest LWB 125 with two-stage supercharging, de Dion rear suspension and four-speed rear-mounted gearbox. In the race he had no better luck than Ascari, his car's transmission failing after 10 laps. Note the twin rear radius rods locating the de Dion tube whereas on the swing-axle cars a single longitudinal rod or fabricated link each side provided fore-and-aft location.

Below right: Swiss Grand Prix, Bremgarten – Sommer's privately-entered Ferrari at Berne was this unsupercharged 2-litre V12 Formula 2 version, a 166, demonstrating yet another Maranello variation upon the theme, with shorter wheelbase but de Dion rear suspension. See its very individual body shape ahead of the rear radius-rod pick-ups; a distinctive car indeed. They all were at this period, each being individually hand-made against the clock by craftsmen of varying ability, and care.

4 June 1950 – Swiss Grand Prix, Bremgarten, Berne – Ferrari had introduced the definitive version of the Gioachino Colombo-designed 1.5-litre supercharged V12 *Tipo* 125 Grand Prix car in the 1949 Italian Grand Prix. Two new long-wheelbase cars there featured de Dion rear suspension in place of the original swing axles, to prevent the tyres up-edging under roll, while new cylinder heads and cam-drives emerged with twin overhead camshafts per cylinder bank. In this form, and in Alfa Corse's 1949 absence, the latest Ferraris were in a class of their own, Ascari's winning easily. Here at Berne, starting the 1950 season, Ascari is practising in a hybrid long-wheelbase model with two-stage supercharged V12 engine, five-speed transmission and the swing-axle rear end. He retired from the Grand Prix after only five laps when an oil pipe parted. Unsupercharged 3.3, later 4.1 and ultimately 4.5-litre *Tipo* 375 cars were on the way which would rapidly replace these complex, costly and thirsty 1500s.

2 July 1950 – *Grand Prix de l'ACF*, Reims-Gueux – Alfa Corse's legendary 'Three-Fs' team made its début in this the Milanese factory team's comeback season. A powerful reason for returning was the introduction of the FIA's new Drivers' World Championship competition. Here they are, the three further developed *Tipo* 158 *Alfetta* cars dominating Reims' front row – Fangio (6), Farina (2), Fagioli (4). But notably, Fangio's pole position time of 2:30.6 was fully 1.9 secs faster than Farina's practice best, and 4.1 secs faster than Fagioli's. Behind them sit the Talbot-Lagos of Étancelin (16), Giraud-Cabantous (18) and Rosier (20), the Maserati 4CLTs of Rol (28) and Argentine newcomer Gonzalez (36); then Parnell's 4CLT (32), Manzon's Simca-Gordini (44) and Claes' Talbot (42). Fangio would win from Fagioli.

Inset: 26 August 1950 – BRDC International Trophy, Silverstone – The great Farina – the driver who popularized more than any other the straight-armed, sit back from the steering wheel driving style – demonstrating the art at the British aerodrome circuit, on which he won both Heat Two and the Final that sunny day, beating his team-mate Fangio. They shared fastest lap at 1:52.0, 96.43 mph. The *Tipo* 158 still retained the distinctive pointed tail with that subtle break in the tail line just around tailpipe level. Note the doubled-up guard over the exhaust to protect the driver's arm from radiant heat, and the green-on-white Alfa Corse team's *Quadrifoglio* badge which doubled as team insignia and good luck symbol. The BRDC required drivers to wear a hard crash helmet that season, but linen helmets would remain more popular until the FIA made crash hats compulsory in 1952.

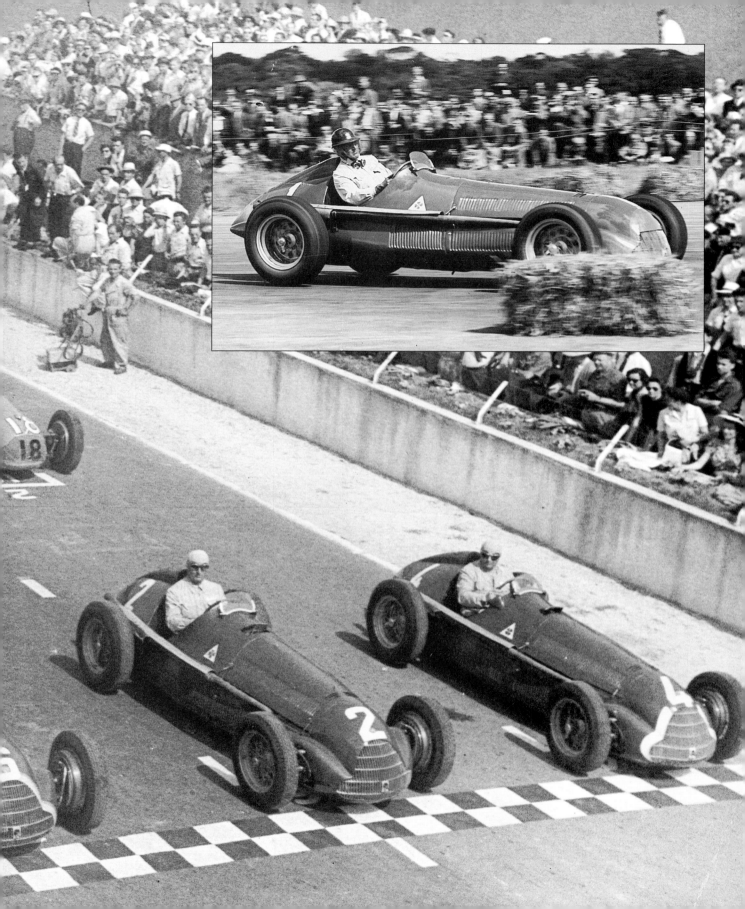

Left: BRDC International Trophy, Silverstone – What the majority of the enormous crowd had come to see that day, race début of the hugely publicized BRM Project 15 (i.e. 1.5-litres) V16-cylinder car – Britain's great white hope for Grand Prix Formula success. Only this one car (of two entered) was air-lifted to Silverstone barely in time to complete three unofficial practice laps to qualify for the Trophy race. After a series of catastrophic engine failures during testing, its power unit had been hastily rebuilt overnight by dog-tired mechanics in the team's workshop at Folkingham Aerodrome in Lincolnshire. The French ace Raymond Sommer had been invited to drive this all-British car. Here he is being push-started on his practice laps – chief mechanic Ken Richardson (in short-sleeved shirt and pullover) to his right, senior engine fitter Dave Turner (overalled) to his left. Note the Porsche-type trailing arm front suspension – *à la* Auto Union and as used on the Mays and Berthon works ERA 'R4D'.

Below left: BRDC International Trophy, Silverstone – The penetrating, full-bodied blast of the BRM V16's spine-tingling exhaust note was about to be heard for the first time in anger before the race-going public. Imagine the anticipation in those as-yet half-empty but soon to be jam-packed grandstands as the start of this race approached. Here Sommer rips by on one of his three exploratory qualifying laps, but in the afternoon – at the moment the race started – his pale-green BRM would snap both its final-drive output shafts and would retire without leaving the startline. Ironically, Sommer had experienced the same fate three years earlier in the French national CTA-Arsenal at Lyons-Parilly. But note the BRM's exquisitely sleek, unlouvred lines, and its build so low that only the tiny headrest projected above the tops of its rear wheels. Aesthetically strong, it was weak on practicalities; to keep that powerful engine cool would demand wholesale butchery of the bodywork.

BRDC International Trophy, Silverstone – BRM backer G.A. 'Tony' Vandervell had become increasingly disenchanted with the cooperative team's slow progress and lack of direction. As a highly successful and autocratic industrialist he chafed against the project's shared command and decision by committee. His patience was ebbing fast. His company's Thin Wall shell bearings were used by Ferrari and in 1949 he had bought an original short-wheelbase, swing-axle *Tipo* 125 with which the BRM team could gain first-hand racing experience. Raymond Mays and Ken Richardson drove it briefly, before the latter crashed, in the British Grand Prix. Now for 1950, 'GAV' replaced it with this new long-wheelbase, two-stage supercharged Ferrari 125 and hired works driver Ascari to handle it in the Trophy race. Painted green with *Thin Wall Special* sign-written on its bonnet, Vandervell's Acton mechanics found the Italians had lettered its cam-boxes *Thinwell Special*. After running badly it spun out of Heat Two during a fierce rain shower. Upon strip-down at Vandervell's Acton factory it was found the bearings had failed due to poor alignment, its bores were oval and scored, rings worn and the crankshaft a maze of hairline cracks. The car was returned to Maranello, while Ferrari mollified Vandervell by fitting one of the new 4½-litre *Tipo* 375 unsupercharged V12s and de Dion rear suspension to give the car a new lease of life for 1951-2.

1951

FERRARI TOPPLES ALFA...

When Ascari won the Peña Rhin Grand Prix in Spain with the new unsupercharged large-capacity Ferrari V12 at the end of 1950, he headed a Ferrari 1-2-3 procession with his friend and mentor Villoresi second in another 4.5-litre *Tipo* 375 and pre-war Gilera motorcycle ace Dorino Serafini third in a 4.1-litre interim version.

At Barcelona, these Ferraris were demonstrably superior in power, speed and handling to the two British BRMs which ran, and the Italian drivers were equally superior in skill to the BRM pairing of Reg Parnell and Peter Walker. Ferrari had won in Alfa Romeo's absence but the manner of their victory gave clear warning to Portello that this new marque was on the march.

During the opening non-Championship races of the 1951 season, they promptly won at Syracuse, Pau and San Remo. *Ing* Lampredi developed a new twin-plug cylinder head for his definitive *Tipo* 375 Formula 1 design, and with some 380bhp allied to modest fuel consumption, Ferrari clearly had a paper advantage over the very latest *Alfetti* whose 404bhp at something like 10,500rpm made them superfast in a straight line, but fuel-bloated and heavy on the startline. They would also need at least two, probably three, refuelling stops to complete race distance.

For years, Alfa Corse had run fast enough between fuel stops to more than compensate for the time lost. In those days, however, the only consistent opposition had been the Talbot-Lagos. Now the new Ferraris could run fast enough to compete with the *Alfetta* on very even terms, and with the Alfas probably requiring at least one more pit stop the writing was clearly on their pit wall. At some stage that season, Ferrari were going to win a *Grande Épreuve* and knock Alfa

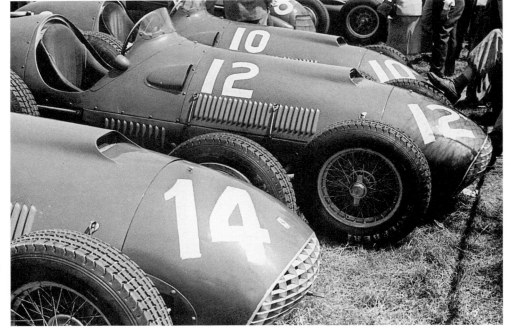

1 July 1951 – *Grand Prix de l'ACF*, Reims-Gueux – The beaten team. Maranello's latest line of Aurelio Lampredi-designed Ferrari 375s with their unsupercharged 4½-litre engines had posed an ever-growing threat to Alfa Corse's predominance during the early part of this new season. Reg Parnell's Vandervell-owned *Thin Wall Special* had been declared the winner at Silverstone in May when torrential rain stopped the International Trophy Final after only 6 laps, but that could hardly count as an Alfa defeat. They then finished 1-3-4 in the Swiss Grand Prix with Taruffi's big Ferrari second. In the minor Ulster Trophy at Dundrod, Farina's Alfa beat Parnell's *Thin Wall*. In the Belgian Grand Prix Farina won from Ferrari 375s 2-3. Then here at Reims-Gueux, Fangio took over Fagioli's Alfa and only just hung on to win from works Ferrari 375s and the *Thin Wall*, 2-3-4. Here in the paddock are – top to bottom – Fagioli's *Alfetta* (8) and the beaten Ferraris of Villoresi (10, third), Ascari (12, gearbox failure, 10 of the 77 laps) and new addition to the team, Gonzalez (14, handed over to Ascari, car finishing second). See how the original aero-screen body shape has been modified with an added coaming, supporting a wrap-round moulded perspex screen, hopefully to improve aerodynamics and minimize cockpit buffeting.

Corse from the lofty perch they had defended so long.

Behind these two great names, the rest of the Formula 1 field amounted to very little. The British BRM consortium was still struggling against over-ambitious design, inefficient management, stringent financial restraints and political infighting. They would only contest the British Grand Prix, and not make a very good showing at it. A later attempt to run two cars at Monza met with abject failure after engine breakage and a minor accident in practice. BRM's consistent failure to start amplified by a needless wrangle over the attempted use of an unrecognized driver at Monza – chief mechanic Ken Richardson – made them a laughing stock. No race promoter anywhere in Europe would trust them to fulfil an entry.

Maserati's 4CLTs were by this time almost universally unreliable makeweights. Their owner-drivers and entrants really did little more than collect the starting money and hope for a fortunate finish and some prize money as a bonus. The surviving Maserati brothers set up their own new OSCA company in 1947, and in 1949 designed a $4\frac{1}{2}$-litre V12 engine commisioned by Amadée Gordini. Gordini was unable to persuade his backers, Simca, to finance the project for Grand Prix racing and later OSCA offered this engine for installation in the 4CLT Maserati chassis. Only 'Bira' was sufficiently keen to buy one. A similarly-engined OSCA Formula 1 car also appeared, purpose-built from scratch, but it only ran in the Italian Grand Prix and flopped.

The makeweights also included the Talbots and Simca-Gordinis from France, the ancient ERAs, newer Altas and the latest 2-litre unblown Formula 2 HWMs from Britain.

Ignoring Indianapolis, the new season's *Grandes Épreuves* were the Swiss, Belgian, French, British, German, Italian and Spanish Grands Prix. During the early part of the year pressure from Ferrari built up relentlessly upon Alfa Corse. At Berne Taruffi's Ferrari split the *Alfetti* of the victorious Fangio and Farina, in second place. At Spa-Francorchamps in the Belgian Grand Prix, Farina hung on to win for Alfa, but Ascari and Villoresi's Ferraris were placed second and third. At Reims for the French Grand Prix there was a battle royal

fought out at staggeringly high speeds between the Fangio, Farina, Fagioli and Sanesi *Alfetti* and the Ferraris of Ascari, Villoresi and a pudgy Argentine newcomer named José Froilan Gonzalez. Fangio took over Fagioli's *Alfetta* to win from Ascari, who likewise had taken over his team-mate Gonzalez's car after his own had failed. Villoresi was third and Parnell fourth in Tony Vandervell's British-entered Ferrari 375, painted green and carrying the *ThinWall Special* logo emblazoned on its bonnet sides. Alfa had won again, but this time the Ferrari fleet finished 2-3-4 in their wake.

The inevitable *dénouement* was reached in the British Grand Prix at Silverstone, where Gonzalez in the Ferrari team's oldest *muletto* car finally put Alfa Romeo to the sword, narrowly beating Fangio after an historic race.

Ascari, who had retired at Silverstone, so liked the look of Gonzalez's winning *muletto* that he demanded it for the subsequent German Grand Prix at Nürburgring. It promptly won again, beating the Alfa *Tipo* 159s then being revamped with stiffened chassis, de Dion rear axles and even more power. A terrific scrap ensued at Monza, where one of the fastest and fiercest Grand Prix races of all time, judged by contemporary standards, was resolved with Ascari victorious for Ferrari from Gonzalez's sister car. Farina was third in the *Alfetta* he had taken over from Felice Bonetto.

The outcome of the World Championship then lay between Fangio of Alfa Romeo and Ascari of Ferrari in the final round, the Spanish Grand Prix at Barcelona. There Ferrari made a fateful tyre choice. They encountered trouble during the race, and Alfa Corse were enabled to win, Juan Fangio leading home Gonzalez to score the first of his record-breaking total of five World Championship of Drivers titles.

The Drivers' table for 1951 finished as follows:

Fangio, World Champion Driver with 31 points
Ascari, 2nd, with 25 points
Gonzalez, 3rd, with 24 points
Farina, 4th, with 19 points
Villoresi, 5th, with 15 points
Taruffi, 6th, with 10 points

Meanwhile, at non-Championship level, 1951 saw 14 other Formula 1 races, of which Ferrari won five (Syracuse, Pau, San Remo, International Trophy Silverstone and Pescara), Alfa Corse three (Ulster Trophy, Bari, Goodwood Trophy), 'Bira's' OSCA the Richmond Trophy, and Maserati the *Grand Prix de Paris* (Farina) and Winfield (Fotheringham-Parker). The Simca-Gordinis won once (at Albi) and Louis Rosier's Talbot-Lago twice – in the Dutch and Bordeaux Grands Prix.

THE CARS COMPETING – 1951

AJB; Alfa Romeo 158 and 159; Grand Prix and F2 Alta; Baird-Griffin; BMW 328; BRM Type 15; Connaught A-Type; Delage *Type Grand Prix* and Delage-ERA; ERA A-Type, B-Type and D-Type; Ferrari 375, 125, 166 and 500; HWM; Jaguar XK120; JP-Vincent; Lea-Francis; Maserati 4CLT; OSCA; RRA; Simca-Gordini; Talbot-Lago T26C

(NB – Some of the decidedly misplaced 'Grand Prix' class cars mentioned above competed only in the Formula 1 Scottish Grand Prix at Winfield Aerodrome, 21 July 1951.)

Right: Grand Prix de l'ACF, Reims-Gueux – A dismayed Ascari bringing in his Ferrari 375 to retire with gearbox failure, this shot showing the identification band added to the car's nose after practice (carefully skirting round the race number), the bonnet-top intake for the carburettors atop the big V12 engine, cockpit cooling duct further back, and the radius rods locating the de Dion tube of the rear suspension.

Opposite top: Grand Prix de l'ACF, Reims-Gueux – There will always be an also-ran; Yves Giraud-Cabantous' venerable Talbot-Lago T26C showing clear evidence of preparation for very hot weather racing; Reims being notorious for its grilling mid-summer temperatures. The French veteran here finished seventh, six laps off the pace. The sister Talbot, with the '*Lago Record*' script lettering on its flanks, appears to be that of Guy Mairesse, who placed ninth on the road but 11 laps behind, too much to classify as a finisher.

Opposite bottom: 14 July 1951 – British Grand Prix, Silverstone – The beaten team. Alfa Corse's fleet of *Alfetta* cars at last succumbed to Ferrari's inexorable pressure and their long years of supremacy were ended by Gonzalez's *muletto* (team hack) 375 this day. Here in the paddock before the race are the cars of Farina (1, caught fire after clutch failure, 75 of the 90 laps); Fangio (2, second behind Gonzalez), Sanesi (3, sixth) and Bonetto (fourth).

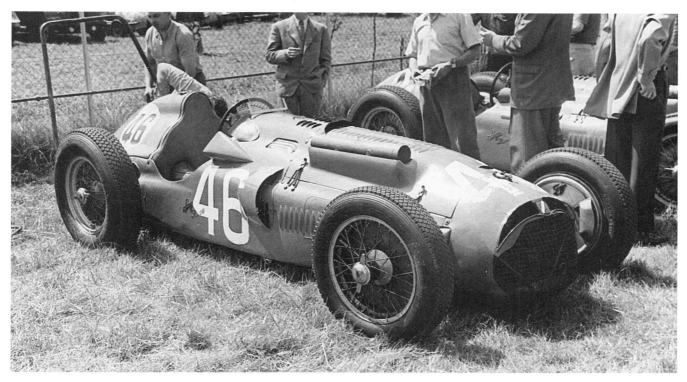

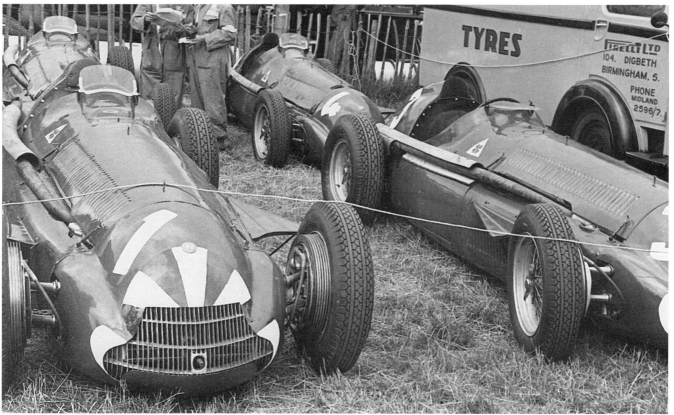

British Grand Prix, Silverstone – Onboard starters were not to become mandatory on Formula 1 cars until 1961. Until that time the best-organised professional teams used portable electric starters such as this, while the rest merely pushed. Just visible on the far side behind the armoured power cable, the starter's reaction foot can be seen resting on the surface of the pit road. The mechanic's thumb is tweaking the starter solenoid and without that starter-foot resting on the ground he would have to be a very strong man indeed to prevent himself being tossed into the car alongside by the starter-motor's torque as it began to kick over that straight-eight engine. The car here is Fangio's (race number 2), showing the two-piece blanking on the radiator grille and its yellow 'edged with dark blue' recognition band. Note the cooling holes in that vast drum brake, the Borrani wire-spoked wheels and Pirelli *Corsa* racing tyres.

Opposite bottom: British Grand Prix, Silverstone – Precision was one of Farina's greatest attributes as a racing driver, although he had another reputation as a man who would ram, nudge, clip and bump aside back-markers without compunction. Here during his abortive pursuit of the Ferraris he aims within millimetres of the sand-filled marker tub, so typical of the British aerodrome circuits of that era. Note the huge heavily-finned drum brakes.

Below: British Grand Prix, Silverstone – Another shot of Farina's *Alfetta*, demonstrating the entirely more bulbous shape and distinctively rounded tail of the large-tanked, fuel-bloated, 410 bhp cars in their 1951 form. Often known as the *Tipo* 159 there is strong factory evidence to suggest that this nomenclature was only given to the revised chassis cars, with extra superstructure stiffening members, which ran in the final Italian and Spanish Grands Prix of Alfa Corse's career. The later *Alfetta* was a surprisingly big and bulky car. From this angle doesn't it make Farina look small?

Overleaf: British Grand Prix, Silverstone – They also serve who only stand and wait; Reg Parnell and Peter Walker handled their still pitifully under-prepared BRM V16s (under-prepared due to more last-minute breakages during final testing, leaving hardly any time for adequate repair) and finished heroically fifth and seventh after dogged and extremely painful drives. The still unlouvred P15 cars' bodies trapped too much under-bonnet heat which was then conducted around poorly-sealed firewall bulkheads back into the cockpit. Both drivers suffered agonising burns and blistering from overheated pedals and general roastingly hot air playing on to their feet and shins. They were also affected, particularly the taller Peter Walker, by inhaling methanol droplets and fumes drawn over and into the cockpit. See how the nose cone had been cut back by this time to improve cooling, but the engine had been detuned considerably to find race-distance reliability. They finished, fifth and seventh, respectively, five and six laps behind Gonzalez's winning Ferrari. As practice failures caused them to non-start in the Italian Grand Prix that September, this would prove to be the BRM V16s' only appearance in any World Championship-qualifying Grand Prix.

Inset: British Grand Prix, Silverstone – Torture chamber; the cockpit in which Reg Parnell was so effectively cooked on his way to an heroic fifth place finish. Visible here are the fuel cock and handbrake lever (to the left) while the gated gearchange can just be seen below the steering wheel rim (right). The rim itself was heavily studded with projections behind to provide grip but the drivers complained bitterly about it being both too close to their chests and too heavily studded, preventing them easily letting it spin through their hands if required. Only the two pitifully small louvres on each side, visible here as two slender vertical lines of light (right), had been provided to cool the depths of the cockpit which was ineffectively sealed against engine-bay air. Note the cowled rearview mirrors and minimal instrumentation – horizontal-strip 12,000 rpm rev counter up front and combination oil pressure and temperature gauge on the after-thought bracket to the left.

British Grand Prix, Silverstone – The British-based Ferrari 375 was Tony Vandervell's 4½-litre *Thin Wall Special* (Peter Whitehead driving here) based on one of the last long-chassis de Dion rear-suspension *Tipo* 125 cars of 1949-50 – actually chassis '125-C-02'. After Ascari had driven it for Vandervell in 1500 cc form in the 1950 International Trophy, the feisty bearings magnate had returned it to Maranello for one of the latest 4½-litre engines to be installed. However, whereas the works 375s for 1951 introduced the new 24-plug V12 engine, Vandervell's was delivered with a 1950-style 12-plug. Even so, engines of this type gave Gonzalez victory in the British Grand Prix and Ascari his win in the German race which followed.

1952

FERRARI'S F2 YEAR

Revolution struck the Grand Prix scene in 1952 as the old pre-war based order was at last overthrown. Formula 1 was effectively abandoned to wither on the vine. In its place, Formula 2, catering for unsupercharged 2-litre racing cars, took precedence and full FIA World Championship status.

Alfa Romeo had been lucky to extricate themselves at the end of 1951 with their second consecutive World Championship title. It was obvious that their immortal *Alfetta* design had reached the limit of practical development. A new design would now be necessary to continue the battle against Ferrari's big unsupercharged V12 cars. The Portello company simply could not justify the expense. When an appeal to the Italian Government failed to attract increased funding specifically to continue Grand Prix racing, Alfa Corse withdrew from Formula 1 and the surviving *Alfetta* cars were consigned to display or storage.

Ferrari found themselves standing alone, on top of an exceedingly small Formula 1 pile. Against their strength, only BRM of England could offer any modern factory-team opposition, but no race promoter other than the tiny French club at Albi and the Ulster AC would trust them. Now, right at the start of the 1952 season, they declined the offer to face Ferrari in the opening non-Championship Formula 1 race at Turin. It was a fatal decision as race promoters across Europe turned to Formula 2 instead, to ensure full grids and an adequate show for paying spectators. Even in Britain, home of the BRM, the RAC and the British Racing Drivers' Club jointly turned to Formula 2 for their major meetings, leaving Formula 1 merely a subsidiary class. The tragedy was that the BRM was on the verge of becoming truly competitive, but the Grand Prix Formula to which it had been built had died while waiting so long for this to happen.

Talbot-Lago of France had long since collapsed. Owners of the big French cars were resigned to running them as make-weights *sans* factory backing and hope. Amedée Gordini was also in his usual parlous financial state as Simca pulled their backing and his team, too, could only struggle forward on a shoestring.

However, since Formula 2's creation in 1948, it had seen four full seasons of good competition. Ferrari had generally dominated, initially using unblown 2-litre *Tipo* 166 versions of the supercharged V12 Grand Prix cars, but at the Modena Grand Prix late in 1951 they introduced Aurelio Lampredi's latest Formula 2 design. Known as the *Tipo* 500, it was a twin-overhead camshaft 4-cylinder of 1980cc. Its simplicity, relatively light weight, good power and considerable mid-range torque made it a nimble and extremely effective road racing car. When the driving skills of Ascari and Villoresi were added the Ferrari 500 was obviously set to achieve great things. For 1952 Ferrari laid down a full team of these cars and more were in production to private customer order.

In response, Maserati made a serious re-entry into the single-seater racing car market with their *Tipo* A6GCM 6-cylinder twin-cam engined car of 1960 cc. This used a 4CLT-type twin-tube chassis with 'live' rear axle, unlike the Ferrari 500's more complex de Dion system. Then Maserati's new driver Fangio crashed and broke his neck at Monza after an all-night drive from his BRM début in Ulster. This put him out for the rest of the season, and Maserati's programme

never properly got into gear.

The indefatigable Italian race engineer and team patron Enrico Platé redeveloped two of his elderly 4CLTs by enlarging their capacity to 1995 cc, removing the original supercharging and cutting-and-shutting the chassis to minimise weight.

Gordini produced new 6-cylinder dohc engines of 1960cc and installed them in neat, redesigned versions of the early 4-cylinder twin-tube chassis. For the first time serious interest was developing in Britain, where John Heath and George Abecassis's HWM team continued to run 4-cylinder Alta engines, and several other constructors turned to the BMW 328-derived Bristol 6-cylinder cross-pushrod power unit. Cooper led this Bristol-engined Formula 2 brigade, while Frazer Nash and the postwar version of ERA also built Bristol-engined Formula 2 cars. Using financial backing from building magnate Kenneth McAlpine, Rodney Clarke and Mike Oliver founded their own line of Connaught single-seater racing cars, having previously begun competition car manufacture with a compact series of Lea-Francis-engined sports cars.

While none of the British engines, Alta, Bristol or Connaught/Lea-Francis, was able to approach the Italians' outright horsepower, Germany (now accepted back into the International racing fold) tried hard with its own BMW-derivatives – the Veritas and the AFM – while Ernst Loof's Veritas concern also developed their own engine later on and Alex von Falkenhausen used the Küchen V8 in his AFM.

While race promoters had rejected Formula 1 because it promised to be a Ferrari walk-over, Formula 2 was in truth little better – it merely had more runners. Ferrari's 500s won every one of the seven World Championship Grands Prix, Ascari utterly dominant with the sole exception of the opening round – the Swiss at Berne – which he missed only because he was racing a Ferrari 375 at Indianapolis (failing to finish due to a wheel collapse). In his absence, Ferrari team-mate Piero Taruffi won instead. The emergent new driver of the season was the tall young Englishman, Mike Hawthorn, whose talent made an under-powered Cooper-Bristol truly competitive with anything but a Ferrari. The 1952 World Championship of Drivers table ended up like this:

Ascari (Ferrari), World Champion Driver with 36 points

Farina, 2nd, with 24 points

Taruffi, 3rd, with 22 points

Rudi Fischer (private Ferrari 500) and Mike Hawthorn (Cooper-Bristol), 4th equal with 10 points each

Robert Manzon (Gordini), 6th, with 9 points

Meanwhile, a very restricted series of five minor Formula 1 races was run that season, in Turin, the Richmond Trophy at Goodwood, the Grand Prix d'Albi, Ulster Trophy at Dundrod and the *Daily Mail* Trophy at Boreham. In addition a number of *Formule Libre* races emerged in which both Formula 1 and Formula 2 cars competed on a virtual *ad hoc* basis. The most important of these was the supporting event for the Formula 2 British Grand Prix at Silverstone. The organising club, the BRDC, had been pressed into scheduling this event by their major sponsors, the *Express* newspaper group. The sole object was to provide a stage upon which the forlorn BRM might at last display its prowess before a home audience. The two V16s entered, for Gonzalez and Wharton, showed prodigious speed, but were beaten by the reliability of Villoresi's Indianapolis-style Ferrari 375.

The Formula 2 Grand Prix class meanwhile saw nearly 30 non-Championship races run throughout the UK and Europe, the most important of which were similarly Ferrari dominated. The French ran a major Formula 2 series paying good money and known as *Les Grands Prix de France*. Ascari's works Ferrari 500s that season won at Syracuse, and then at Pau and Marseilles, in the Monza Autodrome Grand Prix, and at Comminges (with André Simon) and La Baule. His team-mate Villoresi won at Les Sables d'Olonne and Modena, and Piero Taruffi in the *Grand Prix de Paris*. Private Ferrari 500 owner-drivers also shared the swag, the Swiss Rudi Fischer winning the two German 'Rennen – Eifel and AVUS – while Louis Rosier succeeded at Cadours.

Gordini – driven by the irrepressible Jean Behra – beat all the works Ferraris on the super-fast course at Reims and more appropriately on the tight lakeside circuit at Aix-les-Bains. His team-mate Louis Trintignant won at Caen. HWM salvaged victory against non-works opposition at Silverstone (Lance Macklin) and in the *Grand Prix des Frontières* at Chimay (Paul Frère), while Connaught achieved some success in minor UK events late in the season.

Slowly, British constructors were making an impact; Gordini was working wonders with the slenderest resources in France, but Ferrari had very much assumed Alfa Corse's earlier mantle as the *colossus* overshadowing all others.

Opposite top: 14 April 1952 – BARC Goodwood, Easter Monday meeting – A very significant day dawns for British motor racing as the brand-new line-up of Cooper-Bristol T20 Formula 2 cars poses for the cameras before setting the racing world on fire, albeit in a small way. For decades no British single-seater and driver combination had been really competitive, and now the tall blond young man at the end of the line – Mike Hawthorn sitting in Bob Chase's new unpainted car – was about to change all that. Beside him in the white-nosed works prototype Cooper-Bristol is guest driver Fangio, then nearer the camera the two new Écurie Richmond cars of Eric Brandon and Alan Brown. Charles Cooper stands directly behind Fangio, his enthusiastic and dynamic son John sits on the rear wheel of Hawthorn's car. These Mark I Coopers used simple welded-up box-section chassis with twin parallel side members supporting all-independent suspension by high-mounted transverse leafsprings and lower wishbones.

Right: 10 May 1952 – BRDC International Trophy, Silverstone – HWM's fortunes really peaked with luck on their side in this meeting as the Ferrari works entries failed to appear and Lance Macklin and Tony Rolt were able to finish first and second against Gordini and predominantly private-owner opposition in the Final. The effort of running a major four or five car operation entering every available Formula 2 race was literally running HWM's cars, transport and labour force into the ground. Yet their's was still a respected name in Europe. They had achieved an enormous amount for British prestige at a time when BRM's hugely publicized operation could not even guarantee fulfilling entries for a race. This is Tony Rolt's mount, elegantly presented in mid-green..

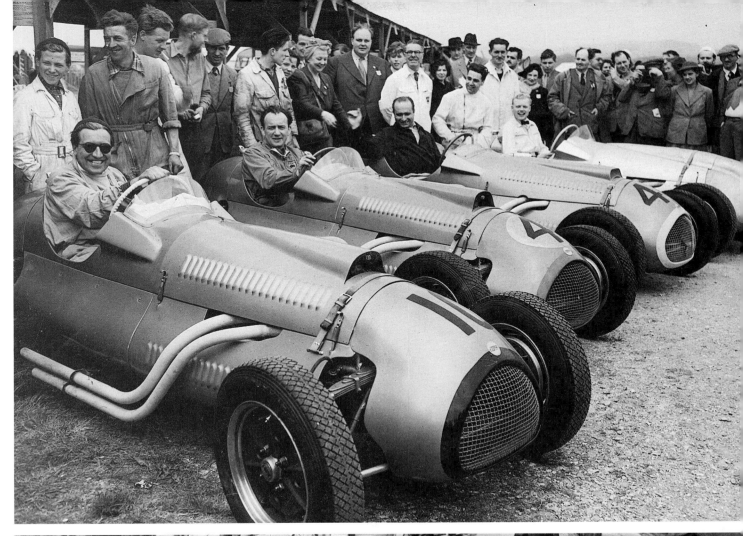

THE CARS COMPETING – 1952

Alta Formula 2 and ex-Grand Prix; Aston-Butterworth; BMW 328; Cisitalia D46; Cooper-Bristol, Cooper-JAP 1000 and 1100, Cooper-NorJAP and Cooper-MG; Connaught A-Type; DB-Panhard; ERA G-Type; Ferrari 500, 166 and 125; FDS; Frazer Nash-Bristol and Le Mans Replica; Gordini; HAR; HWM; HRG-Lea Francis; Jicey-Veritas; Lea-Francis; Lancia *Spéciale*; Maserati A6GCM/52; Maserati-Platé; Monaci; Orly *Special*; OSCA; Paganelli; PS; RRA; Rebrab-JAP; Rover Special; Simca-Gordini; Stanguellini; Veritas-Meteor.

BRDC International Trophy, Silverstone – Gawky newcomers, the AJB Aston-Butterworth Formula 2 project was a brave little operation run by Bill Aston who built himself this neat Formula 2 car powered by inveterate special builder Archie Butterworth's new air-cooled flat-4 engine. He then attracted interest from American Robin Montgomerie-Charrington, who financed the second, similar car parked beyond, which was fitted with the cast light-alloy wheels just visible above No 5. The cars were based upon proprietary Cooper T20-type box-section chassis (as fitted with Bristol engines by the Chase-Hawthorn team, Écurie Richmond etc.), and wore this generally slimmer, taller coachwork with liberal air-cooling vents aft of the engine bay. They achieved very little, eventually retiring, although both survive today – one converted into a sports car and the other still a single-seater.

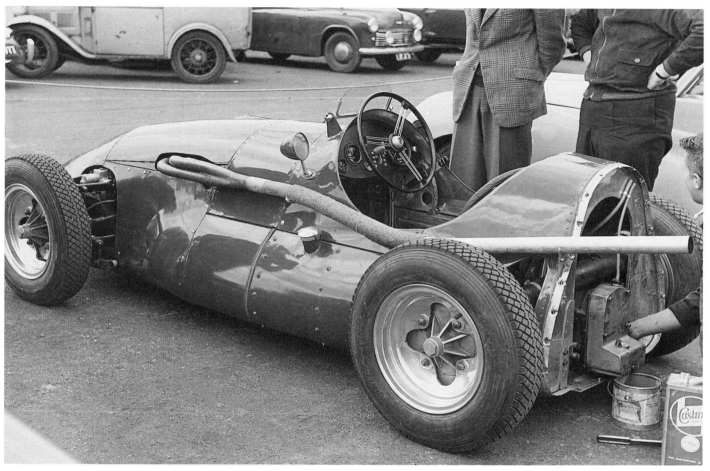

BRDC International Trophy, Silverstone – New shape in the paddocks, Ken Downing's works-entered Connaught A-Type – chassis 'A3' – which unhappily retired after only six laps of Heat One as problems afflicted its Lea-Francis-derived twin-camshaft 4-cylinder engine. Rodney Clarke and Mike Oliver built the most truly sophisticated British racing cars to appear, excepting the perhaps eccentric BRM, prior to Vanwall's début in 1955-6. Backed financially by Kenneth McAlpine of the building company family, they had built a prototype A-Type Formula 2 car for him to race through 1951. Initially using torsion bar-and-wishbone four-wheel independent suspension, the prototype was almost immediately modified by a de Dion rear end, *vide* the de Dion tube arching across the final-drive here. The chassis employed two large-diameter tubular side-members, pannier tanks concentrating fuel load within the wheelbase to minimise handling changes as the load lightened. The pre-selector gear lever is visible in its vertical quadrant by the steering wheel, and do not miss those efficiently-designed, beautifully cast light-alloy wheels. Four more cars like 'A3' joined 'A1' for 1952. Clarke and Oliver progressed to adopt fuel injection, nitromethane fuels, adjustable anti-roll bars and many more fine-tuning tweaks. However, they never had the financial stability to invest in better engines than their own Lea-Francis and later Alta-based units, leaving these somewhat heavy cars as rather staid performers. The rough, tough, simple, lightweight Cooper-Bristols were far more nimble and, in the right hands, faster.

Overleaf main picture: 22 June 1952 – Belgian Grand Prix, Spa-Francorchamps – The shape of things to dominate for two long and (for Ferrari's opposition) tedious years; Alberto Ascari would win the World Championship of Drivers twice in succession and every race he started, or bust in the attempt. Here the lovely lines of Aurelio Lampredi's neat and practical 4-cylinder 2-litre Ferrari 500 are displayed to great advantage, in the dip at Eau Rouge past the pits. It has splash guards fitted behind its front wheels to keep the *Maestro's* elbows reasonably dry and his vision clear, the de Dion rear suspension's twin radius rods are approaching full bump as the rear end loads up in the dip, and note the waterproof wind-cheater which so many self-respecting racing drivers wore in the rain at that time.

Far left inset: Belgian Grand Prix, Spa-Francorchamps – Mike Hawthorn shone brilliantly in this, his maiden *Grande Épreuve*, Bob Chase's Cooper-Bristol by this time wearing a coat of British Racing Green and having been impeccably prepared by Mike's father Leslie and his men at the family's Tourist Trophy Garage in Farnham. Their Bristol engine was tuned to run on an alcohol fuel laced with nitromethane which Leslie himself would mix "back home". Young Mike drove like a tiger in these appalling conditions and actually finished fourth, once lapped by the Ferrari 500s of Ascari and Farina, and by Robert Manzon's quick Gordini. See how far he towers out of the little Cooper's cockpit. His visor was vital as much to enable him to breathe in the fume-laden atmosphere as to see.   **52/6**

Left inset: Belgian Grand Prix, Spa-Francorchamps – Ken Wharton drove very well to keep contact with Hawthorn in this Peter Bell-owned, Scuderia Franera-entered Frazer Nash Formula 2 single-seater. The Isleworth company had produced a very successful line of Bristol-engined Le Mans Replica sports cars, and the narrow Mark II twin-tube chassis was ideal for completion as a centralized single-seater. The Frazer Nash Formula 2 cars involved a literal case of "An Englishman, an Irishman and a Scotsman" as Peter Bell had commissioned Wharton's car on chassis '421/200/172' with an 'S' suffix added for single-seater. Its bonnet-top carburettor-air trunking won it the nickname 'The Wharton Whale'. Two similar cars were built subsequently for Scotsman Bill Kelly and Irishman Dickie Odlum to use mainly at club level. Here at Spa on this damp day, Wharton was very lucky to escape without serious hurt after losing control on the slippery surface and having his wind-cheater torn by the top strand of a barbed wire fence as he spun beneath it. Racing was a risky business . . .

19 July 1952 – British Grand Prix, Silverstone – Gino Bianco in one of the Brazilian *Escuderia Bandeirantes* team's Maserati A6GCMs heading towards a tardy eighteenth place, eight laps off Ascari's winning pace in the works Ferrari. The A6GCM was a small, relatively light and conventional car of the period with twin-tube chassis and 6-cylinder double overhead camshaft engine. Twelve were built, chassis numbered '2032' to '2038', then '2041', '44', '46', '48' and '2051'. Most were eventually sold, as was normal Maserati practice, to private owners who continued to race them with varying degrees of factory technical support and backing. Heitel Cantoni's Brazilian team bought the first two and effectively also-ran them in a full Formula 2 season. Further development was vital to make them competitive, but Maserati's own works team's plans for this season were wrecked when Fangio broke his neck in an A6GCM at Monza and was effectively sidelined for the whole season.

British Grand Prix, Silverstone – One of the saddest sights in 1952-3 was that of Stirling Moss struggling to make his mark in inadequate British-built cars. While Mike Hawthorn was about to attract and would sensibly accept the offer of a Ferrari works drive for 1953, Moss' earlier similar approach from Ferrari had ended in long estrangement. Essentially, Moss's ambition was to beat the red cars in one wearing British green, but until 1957 none would be consistently and sufficiently competitive to do the job. This David Hodkin-designed G-Type ERA embodied many advanced ideas, being based upon an essentially twin-tube frame rolled from magnesium-sheet for minimum weight and incorporating low polar moment of inertia concentration of major masses within its wheelbase. It was Bristol-engined, offset-seated to double as a sports car, a redundant facility as it transpired, and it proved both less driveable and slower than even the simplest Cooper-Bristols. Here Moss retired after 36 laps with a blown cylinder-head gasket. The G-Type project was eventually sold to Bristol Cars, to found their successful 2-litre class Le Mans Coupé programme.

3 August 1952 – German Grand Prix, Nürburgring – Shadows of the Silver Arrows lay pretty thin postwar until the re-emergence of Daimler-Benz in 1954. Best of the bunch were undoubtedly the BMW-derived Veritas cars built by Ernst Loof, formerly an engineer in BMW's works racing department at Munich. Initially he simply race-prepared Type 328 sports cars whose specification just pre-war had been startlingly futuristic and which had achieved widespread success in all kinds of competition. He progressed to building Formula 2 cars from basic 328s supplied by customers, then built his own sports and

Formula cars from scratch. He even redesigned the famous cross-pushrod, alloy-head 6-cylinder engine, on which the British Bristol unit was based, to have true Veritas engines built for him by Heinkel. Here is Hans Klenk, a sometime Mercedes-Benz works driver until he was hurt very severely in a testing accident, heading his early-series Veritas towards retirement on lap 14 of the GP.

German Grand Prix, Nürburgring – The Australian private owner Tony Gaze acquired this ex-works 1951-type HWM and raced it with a measure of HW Motors' support through the 1952 Formula 2 season. Here he survived six laps until his car's pre-selector gearbox failed. The metallic mid-green paint on the car here is highlighted by that Australian gold stripe around its torso; possibly another very attractive subject for the racing car model maker.

1953

THE TRIDENT FIGHTS BACK

Ferrari encountered stiffer opposition during this second season of World Championship Formula 2 racing as Maserati's 6-cylinder A6GCM/53 was a far better car than its predecessor of 1952 and the driving skills of Juan Fangio and Froilan Gonzalez in the Trident cars' cockpits pressurized Ascari as never before. The Maseratis and Ferrari 500s were very evenly matched, with the 4-cylinder Maranello cars having an edge on the slower circuits and greater reliability.

Chasing the Italians, Cooper introduced a more sophisticated curved-tube spaceframe version of their Bristol-engined Formula 2 design – to replace the original twin box-section chassis. Some customers adopted Alta engines instead of the Bristol. HWM developed their own cylinder head for the basically Alta engine but were losing their grip by this stage as the competitiveness of Formula 2 finally swamped their meagre resources.

Mike Hawthorn's exploits in his Bob Chase-owned Cooper-Bristol prepared by his father Leslie in 1952 had won him a drive with Ferrari. He made his début for them in the inaugural World Championship-qualifying Argentine Grand Prix in January, 1953, and in mid-summer won the French Grand Prix, beating Fangio and Gonzalez of Maserati to the line. This was a stunning boost to British motor racing pride as he became the first Briton since Henry Segrave in 1923 to win a *Grande Épreuve*. What British enthusiasts wanted now was for a home-grown driver to repeat that success in a home-grown car. They had another four years to wait.

Once again Alberto Ascari's Ferraris dominated the World Championship series, winning the Argentine, Dutch, Belgian, British and Swiss Grands Prix. Hawthorn added victory at Reims-Gueux, Farina won the German Grand Prix for Ferrari and then – after a dramatic race-long duel culminating in a final corner multiple collision – Fangio won the Italian Grand Prix for Maserati. Ferrari dominance had at last been dented.

The 1953 World Championship of Drivers result looked like this:

Ascari, (Ferrari), World Champion Driver with $34\frac{1}{2}$ points
Fangio (Maserati), 2nd, with 28 points
Farina (Ferrari), 3rd, with 26 points
Hawthorn (Ferrari), 4th, with 19 points
Villoresi (Ferrari), 5th, with 17 points
Gonzalez (Maserati), 6th, with $13\frac{1}{2}$ points

THE CARS COMPETING – 1953

AFM; Formula 2 Alta; Aston-Butterworth; BMW 328; Connaught A-Type; Cooper-Bristol T20 and T23, Cooper-MG and Cooper-JAP; Cromard-Lea Francis Special; DHS-Rover; Emeryson-Alta and Emeryson-Aston Martin; Ferrari 500,553 and 166; Frazer Nash Formula 2 and Le Mans Replica; Gordini *Type* 16; HAR; HWM; IRA-Bristol; Jicey; Kieft-Bristol and Kieft-JAP; Maserati A6GCM/52 and A6GCM/53; Monnier-BMW *Spéciale*; OSCA; RRA; Tojeiro-Bristol; Turner-Lea Francis; Veritas.

Opposite top: 18 January 1952 – Argentine Grand Prix, Buenos Aires autodrome – Start of the new year's World Championship-opening three-hour Grand Prix with the all-Italian front rows surging into battle; Mike Hawthorn making his début for Ferrari taking a brief lead (right, number 16), from Villoresi (Ferrari 500, centre, 14), followed by Farina (Ferrari 500, 10), Gonzalez (Maserati A6GCM, 4), Ascari (Ferrari 18), Fangio (left, Maserati A6GCM, 2) Bonetto (right, Maserati A6GCM, 6). Behind him are Oscar Galvez in the hired fourth works Maserati, then the Gordinis of Behra and Menditeguy, etc.

Right: 9 May 1953 – BRDC International Trophy, Silverstone – Mike Hawthorn's prodigious and precocious talents having been signed-up by Ferrari, the Cooper-Bristol banner was best waved this season by Ken Wharton who is seen here in his latest style multi-tubular framed Cooper-Bristol Type 23. This car was progressively well developed and Wharton became easily the best of the 'second division' British drivers, behind the cream of the new postwar generation like Hawthorn, Moss and Collins. Here the Cooper's transverse leafspring all-independent suspension is clearly visible, together with its simple uprights, finned drum brakes, narrow cast-alloy wheels and telescopic dampers picking-up halfway along the lower suspension wishbones. Wharton finished second behind Hawthorn's Ferrari in Heat Two, then fifth in the Final.

21 June 1953 – Belgian Grand Prix, Spa-Francorchamps – On the very fast Ardennes public road circuit Maserati's strikingly sleek new 6-cylinder A6GCM/53 cars had the legs of Ferrari's hitherto all-conquering 4-cylinder 500s. Fangio took pole position in this car, his team-mate Gonzalez sandwiching Ascari's Ferrari on the front row. They both out-accelerated it from the start and until one-third distance it looked as if Maserati must win at last. Then Gonzalez's leading A6GCM broke its transmission, and Fangio's its engine. Belgian guest driver Johnny Claes was called in for Fangio to take

over his car, and the Argentinian had worked his way back into third place only to spin off on the last lap. Just as Ferrari had done to Alfa Romeo in 1951, Maserati was relentlessly pressuring Ferrari ever harder throughout 1953 – finally winning in their own Italian Grand Prix at Monza. Fangio's car seen here in the Spa pits is brand spanking new, in lovely order. See the Trident emblem on its scuttle side and the grille bars spread on the right side to enable a portable starter shaft to pass through.

18 July 1953 – British Grand Prix, Silverstone – Fangio demonstrating his peerless car control in the works Maserati A6GCM/53 – chassis '2046' – at Becketts' Corner, tightest on the aerodrome course, while chasing the inevitable Ascari's Ferrari. He finished second while his team-mate Gonzalez shared fastest lap with the reigning World Champion's 500.

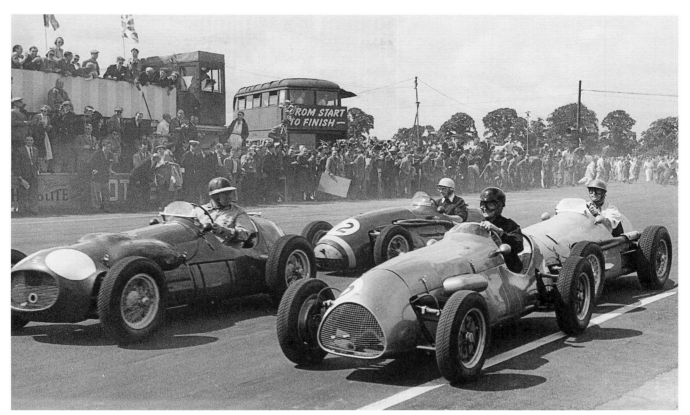

British Grand Prix, Silverstone – Tangle at the back of the grid as Duncan Hamilton's latest 1953-style HWM falters, Tony Crook (dark helmet) dodges by in his Cooper-Alta Mark II – with the multi-tubular chassis replacing the original twin box-section 1952-style used in the original Cooper-Bristol Mark 1s – on this side with Louis Rosier's private Ferrari 500 following through. Beyond, Roy Salvadori opts for the far side with his works A-Type Connaught. Of this group only Rosier would finish, unclassified, 12 laps behind Ascari's basically similar but works-prepared and entered winning Ferrari, Rosier thus effectively eleventh and last.

2 August 1953 – German Grand Prix, Nürburgring – the *Sudkehre* 'roundabout' corner on the opening lap with a truly representative field of the season's Formula 2 Grand Prix cars turning in; Fangio (Maserati A6GCM/53, No 5), leading the way followed by Ascari (Ferrari 500, 1), Hawthorn (Ferrari 500, 3), de Graffenried (A6GCM/53, 17), Bonetto (A6GCM/53, 7), Trintignant's Gordini (on the outside), Villoresi's and Farina's Ferrari 500s and – again on the outside line – Behra's Gordini. The rest are led by Alan Brown's Cooper-Bristol.

German Grand Prix, Nürburgring – Another view of the Ernst Loof-built Veritas, this 1953 version being Theo Helfrich's Formula 2 car – one of nine variegated examples of the marque entered amongst this German Grand Prix's enormous 34-strong field. Helfrich finished twelfth, 45 kms (28 mls) behind Farina's winning Ferrari. In 1952, he and Niedermayer had co-driven a works Mercedes-Benz 300SL Coupé into second place behind the victorious sister car of Lang and Riess at Le Mans.

1954

DAIMLER–BENZ RETURNS

A new set of 2½-litre Formula 1 regulations took effect from 1 January 1954, catering for single-seater racing cars with unsupercharged engines, no less than 2-litres, but including a supercharged category for engines of between 500 and 750 cc. Not surprisingly, nobody other than DB-Panhard seriously attempted the supercharged route, and here at last was a truly post-war purpose-built Grand Prix Formula.

The most significant feature of this maiden season was the re-emergence of Daimler-Benz on the Grand Prix scene. The German manufacturer had reappeared in International sports car racing in 1952, when the gull-wing *Typ* 300SL Coupé cars won the Le Mans 24-Hours race. When the new 2½-litre Formula 1 had been announced by the CSI the Daimler-Benz board in Stuttgart had quickly authorized design and construction of a suitable team. In parallel an associated long-distance sports-racing car design was to be developed to tackle the Sports Car World Championship title inaugurated in 1953.

The new Daimler-Benz *Rennabteilung* was not ready to race until the French Grand Prix in mid-summer at Reims-Gueux. In order to buy off potential opposition, Daimler-Benz had wisely contracted the best driver available, Juan

Fangio, but until their cars appeared he was allowed to continue with Maserati through the first two Grands Prix, which of course he won, in Argentina and Belgium.

Ascari and his inseparable friend and mentor Villoresi had meanwhile signed-up with Gianni Lancia's forthcoming Formula 1 team but their Vittorio Jano-designed and highly sophisticated potential Mercedes-killers were not to appear until right at the end of the 1954 season, in the Spanish Grand Prix at Barcelona.

Meantime Ascari, the reigning World Champion, actually missed the Argentine and Belgian Grands Prix, before campaigning one of the new Maserati 250Fs in the French event and qualifying it on the outside of the front row. Standing alongside him were Fangio and his German team-mate Karl Kling in the staggering new streamlined-bodied Mercedes-Benz W196s. Ascari also ran a Maserati in the British Grand Prix and a Ferrari in the Italian event before Lancia provided him with a car capable of matching his wasted skills, and potentially of meeting Daimler-Benz on level terms.

The new Mercedes used a complex roller-bearing straight-eight cylinder engine featuring fuel injection and desmodromic (positively opened and closed) valves. It developed some 272 bhp at 8000 rpm. At Reims and in the British Grand Prix at Silverstone the cars ran with wheel-enveloping streamlined bodies, but after tyre problems, associated lack of grip and a lot of marker-tub thumping at Silverstone a more conventional open-wheeled slipper type body was introduced in time for the German Grand Prix at Nürburgring.

Meanwhile, Maserati developed the 250F 6-cylinder – for many the absolute epitome of the postwar front-engined Grand Prix car – from their experience with the A6GCM/53, and it won straight out of the box in Fangio's peerless hands. However, upon his switch to Mercedes on the début of their more powerful cars, Maserati fortunes tumbled. Their saving grace was the large number of 250Fs sold to private owners, including that other very promising young Englishman, Stirling Moss.

Ferrari lost its way after its two dominant seasons of 1952-3 and as more money and resources were being devoted to sports-racing and production car development so Ferrari's Formula 1 spearhead for the new class was a rather half-hearted looking *Tipo* 625 update on the old *Tipo* 500 theme. This used the 4-cylinder dohc engine now in 2490cc form. A more radical rethink was also under development in the side-tanked *Squalo* or 'Shark' model, the *Tipo* 553 which had first emerged in Formula 2 form in the 1953 Italian Grand Prix but whose handling peculiarities counted heavily against it, hence the 625 update as insurance.

Foreign opposition was confined by financial restraints to Gordini uprating his 6-cylinder Formula 2 engine to 2473cc. HWM did a similar job, Connaught adopted a 4-cylinder 2½-litre Alta engine gas-flowed by Harry Weslake; while Tony Vandervell, erstwhile disgruntled backer of the BRM project, fielded his *Vanwall Special* for the first time with a 4-cylinder engine derived from the 500cc Norton racing motorcycle cylinder design mated to a Rolls-Royce B40 military engine-inspired crankcase. This car used a Cooper-designed tubular chassis and had been intended to compete in Formula 2 as a 2-litre. However, its development had taken considerably longer than scheduled. When first raced in 1954 it was handicapped by having only a 2-litre engine which was rapidly enlarged, first to 2.3 and finally to 2.5-litres. Tony Vandervell lavished every resource and expense upon this car which was clearly a serious project aimed unswervingly at beating all opposition. It would take time – but Vanwall would prevail.

The 1954 World Championship of Drivers top six were:

Fangio (Maserati and Mercedes-Benz), World Champion Driver with 42 points
Gonzalez (Ferrari), 2nd, with 25⅐ * points
Hawthorn (Ferrari), 3rd, with 24 9/14 points
Trintignant (Ferrari), 4th, with 17 points
Kling (Mercedes-Benz), 5th, with 12 points
Herrmann (Mercedes-Benz), 6th equal, with 8 points (tied by Bill Vukovich, winner of the Indianapolis 500 which was still officially a World Championship round).

These silly fractions of a point came about through the RAC using egg-timers of such poor accuracy at the British Grand Prix that they could not separate seven drivers for fastest lap, which in those days was worth an extra Championship point. When Hawthorn later shared another fastest lap with one other driver to add his seventh of a point from Silverstone we find ourselves reduced to 14ths of a point as the common factor.

Some 24 non-Championship Formula 1 races (of all levels) were run, of which Mercedes won the only one they contested, the *AVUSRennen* (Karl Kling).

Ferrari's 625s won at Syracuse (Farina), Bordeaux and Bari (Gonzalez) and Rouen and Caen (Trintignant), while in England Reg Parnell's private version revived the old Scuderia Ambrosiana team title and won twice each at Goodwood and Crystal Palace and once at Snetterton.

The Maserati 250Fs also won their share – at Snetterton (Salvadori), Rome (Marimon), Chimay ('Bira' in an interim A6GCM fitted with a 250F engine) and Pescara (Luigi Musso) while Moss' cars won at Oulton Park, Goodwood and Aintree (Moss).

Finally Gordini, thanks largely to Jean Behra, won at both Pau and Cadours. It had been a hectic first season for the new 2½-litre Formula.

THE CARS COMPETING – 1954

Connaught A-Type; Cooper-Bristol T20 and T23, Cooper-JAP and Cooper-Vincent; DHS; Emeryson-Alta and Emeryson-Aston Martin; Ferrari 625 and 555; Giaur-Fiat; Gordini; Griefzu-BMW Special; HAR; HWM; Klenk-Meteor; Lancia D50; Maserati 250F and A6GCM/250; Mercedes-Benz W196; RRA; Vanwall Special; Turner-Alta; Veritas.

15 May 1954 – BRDC International Trophy, Silverstone – For this first season of 2½-litre Formula 1 racing, Ferrari developed a double-pronged approach; one the latest Lampredi-designed 4-cylinder *Squalo* design with midship fuel tankage as introduced in the Formula 2 *Tipo* 553 model at Monza, 1953; and the other the installation of enlarged 2½-litre engines in the old faithful 500 chassis, to produce the Ferrari 625. Here in the BRDC May meeting at Silverstone, Gonzalez, back at Ferrari after two seasons with Maserati, won Heat One in 553/2 (seen here) only for its engine to seize on the warm-up lap for the Final. He promptly took over Trintignant's 625, which had won Heat Two, and duly dominated the Final.

Opposite top: BRDC International Trophy, Silverstone – What should have emerged in 1953 as the Formula 2 *Vanwall Special* finally made its delayed début here driven by Alan Brown. Tony Vandervell had finally despaired of BRM ever achieving anything concrete, his own Formula 1 *Thin Wall Special* Ferrari was effectively confined to national club racing, yet as a Director of Norton he was anxious to reproduce their World Championship motor-cycling success on four wheels. At his instigation, a Formula 2 engine was developed based around the idea of four 500 cc Norton motorcycle-inspired cylinder barrels mounted upon a Rolls-Royce commercial engine-derived crankcase, fuel injected by the best system currently available. On its début here, with later Vanwall and BRM chief mechanic Cyril Atkins warming it up, the new car, still in 2-litre form, featured an ungainly gilled-tube surface radiator. Alan Brown finished sixth in Heat One and retired from the Final with a broken oil pipe after 17 of 35 laps.

Right: BRDC International Trophy, Silverstone – Gone foreign – when Stirling Moss's enthusiastic backers proposed to Daimler-Benz that it should hire his services for the new Formula, Stuttgart racing director Alfred Neubauer retorted that Moss should first "prove himself in a decent car – buy a Maserati". Stirling's father and his manager Ken Gregory did just that, and here he is seen cornering this so-beautiful front-engined Italian Grand Prix car in second place in the Final before its de Dion tube snapped after 25 of 35 laps. These new *Tipo* 250F cars were derived directly from A6GCM/53 experience and in Fangio's hands the works' number one car won first time out in Argentina, then again in the Belgian Grand Prix. The side filler cap betrays the original engine-bay mounting of the dry-sump oil tank, soon after transferred to the extreme tail, while Moss's personal superstitions are revealed by the horseshoe and his lucky number 7.

4 July 1954 – *Grand Prix de l'ACF*, Reims-Gueux – Dawn of a new era as Mercedes-Benz's formidable *Rennabteilung* returned to the Grand Prix fray with this stunning new W196 2½-litre design, complete with central-seat, all-enveloping *Stromlinienwagen* aerodynamic coachwork. The W196 – 'W' for *Wagen* (car) used the M196 – 'M' for *Motoren* – engine, a slant-mounted straight-eight with central power take-off between cylinders nos 4 and 5 to minimise crankshaft torsional vibration problems, plus sophisticated desmodromic valvegear. This power-unit drove to a rear-mounted transaxle. Low-pivot swing axle rear suspension was well-tamed and with Mercedes-Benz's formidable facilities, virtually no stone had been left unturned in design and construction. Continental racing tyres were not the equal of Pirelli as used by Maserati but with Mercedes taking up their pre-arranged option on Fangio he left the Italian team to join them and some Italians never really forgave him for it . . . This is his car, chassis 'W196/00003', in the grass paddock behind the Reims-Gueux pits, and on its way to the startline, immediately before starting this début race from pole position, and winning handsomely just under 2hrs 43mins later.

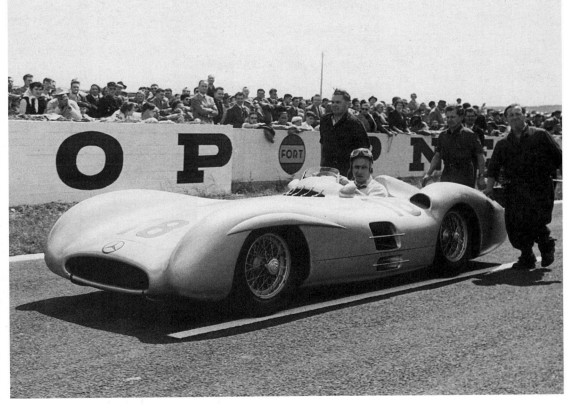

26 October 1954 – Spanish Grand Prix, Pedralbes circuit, Barcelona – In sunnier climes than Silverstone, Mercedes stuttered again, the hot wind off the Mediterranean throwing up clouds of litter along the main straight which blocked the radiator intakes of the German cars, exacerbating already marginal cooling. As the open-wheeler bodied W196 cars of Fangio and Kling faltered, and young Hans Herrmann's suffered injection trouble, Mike Hawthorn was able to win his second Grand Prix for Ferrari, in the much improved revised-suspension *Squalo* here seen opposite-locking away from one of the slower corners.

Spanish Grand Prix, Barcelona – A perfect comparison here as Fangio tries both his open-wheeler slipper-bodied Mercedes-Benz W196 and its *Stromlinienwagen* sister during back-to-back practice testing. In the race he drove the open-wheeled car – chassis '0008' – eventually finishing third. Kling was fifth and Herrmann retired the third *Silberpfeil*.

Spanish Grand Prix, Barcelona –
Threatening newcomer, and an
exquisitely-made new Italian
Formula 1 car which could
possibly have toppled Mercedes'
supremacy had luck been on its
side, which it was not. This is
the first Lancia D50 to appear,
driven in practice by Alberto
Ascari, eager to get back into the
fray. He did it well enough in his
assigned race car to qualify
resoundingly on pole position, a
whole second faster than Fangio's
W196. He then led the opening
stages of the race, until a leaking
oil seal and clutch failure forced
retirement on lap 10 of the
scheduled 80. Here the side-
tanked D50's very compact
packaging is emphasised by the
bulky figure of Ascari in its
cockpit. 'L' for *leather*, perhaps?

Spanish Grand Prix, Barcelona –
The gleaming new Lancia D50
here shows off its
comprehensively machined and
polished mechanical finish, tube
outriggers supporting the side
tanks, deeply finned brake drums,
streamlined flaps covering fuel
and oil tank fillers on the stubby
tail, simple, ergonomically-efficient
dash panel design, right-hand
gearchange and comfy padding
for the driver's shoulders.

Spanish Grand Prix, Barcelona – In lieu of a BRM, the Owen Racing Organisation (which had owned the 'British Racing Motor' project since 1952) fielded its self-developed and extensively modified Maserati 250F – nominally chassis '2509' – to be driven by the faithful Ken Wharton. When development engineer Tony Rudd found the multi-tubular chassis as delivered woefully lacking in torsional rigidity, he had several extra bracing members inserted, achieving a considerable improvement when measured on the test rig, if not so conclusively perhaps on the race track. The car was further fitted with the latest Dunlop perforated disc alloy wheels and its engine was carefully rebuilt and re-prepared. Finished in British Racing Green this Owen Maserati went quite well without ever challenging the Modenese factory cars, though Peter Collins would win the 1955 International Trophy with it at Silverstone. Here Wharton finished a distant eighth, six laps off the pace.

1955
LANCIA DIE, MERCEDES PREVAIL...

This was absolutely the season of Mercedes-Benz. Daimler-Benz's racing manager Alfred Neubauer signed up Stirling Moss to join Fangio and Kling as the backbone of his Formula 1 team. Their only near rival was Lancia Corse, whose parent company finally succumbed to financial decline coinciding with the death of Alberto Ascari in a casual Ferrari sports car drive at Monza. The result, as Maserati proved incapable of competing with the German teams on engine and driver power, was a walk-over

season – save a minor hiccup at Monaco – for the crushing superiority of Germany's finest.

This 1955 season was riven by tragedy. By far the worst single incident was the Le Mans disaster, in which a Mercedes-Benz 300SLR sports-racing car crashed at high speed in front of the main spectator area opposite the pits. Over 80 died in addition to the driver 'Levegh' as the crashing car's engine, front suspension and other debris hurtled through the crowd.

Shock waves resounded throughout the motor sporting world. The French Government immediately banned all motor racing, as did the Swiss. Once safety provisions at race circuits had been re-appraised the French permitted racing to resume. The Swiss did not, and only one-car-at-a-time hill-climbs and rallying are permitted in the Cantons even today. The year's German and Spanish Grands Prix were both cancelled and improved protective safety banks around circuits became compulsory both in Europe and in the UK. Many of the old traditional public road circuits were lost as promoting clubs could not afford the modifications necessary, or failed to agree new requirements with local police authorities and insurers.

Discounting Indianapolis, the Drivers' World Championship series of Grands Prix was thus slashed to just six, of which Mercedes won five, losing only at Monaco where a minor valve gear component fault cost them dear and where the unfortunate Alberto Ascari crashed his Lancia D50 into the harbour at the moment of inheriting the lead. He was killed in a Ferrari *Monza* sports car at the Milanese Autodrome the following Wednesday, having merely taken it out for a casual run to test reactions after his ducking.

At Monaco, Trintignant had won in a 4-cylinder Ferrari 625 version of the double-Championship winning 500 design. Fangio became Champion for the third time. Lancia withdrew from serious competition after Monaco, Castellotti running one car only at Spa as a quasi-privateer and proving that it was the equal – at least in outright performance – of the German cars until it broke, which the Mercedes so seldom did.

Ferrari was spreadeagled by Mercedes, Maserati's 250Fs were more modern but lacked the luck to win, and by the time of the Italian Grand Prix, Lancia had ceded the racing department hardware to Ferrari. This stunning windfall, plus the promise of financial assistance from Fiat to continue racing for *la patria*, was to revive Ferrari fortunes.

Short-term, however, the Lancia D50s which Ferrari ran in practice on the new combined banked and road circuit at Monza simply ate tyres. Ferrari was contracted to Englebert, and supplies of Pirelli tyres to which the D50 had been specifically tailored, were cut off. Shredding Englebert treads then created savage vibration which eventually burst the casings at high speed. Farina's D50 burst a tyre at 170-plus and spun for half a mile. There was a repeat performance next day. Sensibly, Ferrari then withdrew its new Lancias and relied upon its own obsoles-

cent armament instead. Against the latest Mercedes on race day there was no contest; the German cars finished first and second.

Then, right at the close of this fraught season, the remote non-Championship Formula 1 race at Syracuse in Sicily provided a true sporting sensation. Against a full Maserati field, Tony Brooks – an amateur driver deep into studies as a dental surgeon – beat them all in his works-entered B-Type Connaught. Driver and team thus became the first all-British combination to win a major-Formula European Grand Prix since Segrave and Sunbeam had succeeded at San Sebastian in 1924. As Rodney Walkerley, Sports Editor of *The Motor* put it: ". . . a straw in the wind that was soon to become a gale."

Another event of singular importance that October was the Daimler-Benz announcement that they were retiring from racing forthwith. Their 300SLR sports-racing cars had just won the Targa Florio to clinch the Sports Car World Championship in addition to their Drivers' title. It was an opportune time to stop.

Ferrari perked up at the news. Work began to 'Maranellize' its Lancia D50 windfall. Maserati buckled down to a hard winter's work which would produce cars capable of winning both Formula 1 and Sports Car World Championship titles. In England, BRM had a new 4-cylinder $2\frac{1}{2}$-litre car – the Project 25 – showing terrific pace and great promise. Vanwall also showed good pace, despite myriad niggling problems. Connaught had just proved they could win, while Gordini was developing a true Formula 1 straight-8 despite having become an underfinanced also-ran.

The 1955 World Championship of Drivers final table was like this:

Fangio (Mercedes-Benz), World Champion Driver with 40 points
Moss (Mercedes-Benz), 2nd, with 23 points
Castellotti (Lancia and Ferrari), 3rd, with 12 points
Trintignant (Ferrari), 4th, with $11\frac{1}{3}$ points
Farina (Ferrari), 5th, with $10\frac{1}{3}$ points
Taruffi (Ferrari and Mercedes-Benz), 6th, with 9 points

At non-Championship level, Lancia's ultimately fatal European season had begun with great promise as Ascari had won at Turin and Naples. Maserati's 250Fs had won at Goodwood,

Snetterton and Aintree (Salvadori in Syd Greene's Gilby Engineering car), at Crystal Palace (Hawthorn in Moss's), Pau and Bordeaux (Behra's works entries), Silverstone (Collins in the BRM team's modified Owen Maserati), Albi (André Simon) and Oulton Park (Moss). And then there was the emergent new Vanwall team in Britain, for which Harry Schell won twice – at Snetterton and Castle Combe. Add that great Connaught victory at Syracuse and the balance was imperceptibly changing.

THE CARS COMPETING – 1955

Arzani-Volpini; Berkshire Special (Lea-Francis); BRM P25; Connaught A-Type and B-Type; Cooper-Alta and Cooper-Bristol (includes Jack Brabham's rear-engined prototype); DB-Panhard supercharged 750; Emeryson-Alta; Ferrari 625, 555 and 166; Gordini; HAR; HWM; Lancia D50; Lister-Bristol; Lotus-Bristol Mark IX; Maserati 250F and A6GCM/250; Mercedes-Benz W196; Turner-Alta; Vanwall.

22 May 1955 – Monaco Grand Prix, Monte Carlo – Lancia Corse's last great hurrah, with their fleet of four exquisite V8-engined D50 cars lined-up ready for battle on the paved Monaco quayside. Number '32' in the foreground had been entrusted to Monégasque Champion Louis Chiron who, in his mid-fifties, was about to become the oldest driver ever to compete in a *Grande Épreuve*. A stirring Lancia drive in the Monte Carlo Rally had won him this final opportunity to demonstrate his polished skills. The D50s beyond were to be driven by Eugenio Castellotti, Luigi Villoresi and Alberto Ascari, who would plunge into the harbour on the lap in which he should have inherited the lead, Moss's Mercedes having just expired at the pits.

16 July 1955 – British Grand Prix, Aintree – The story of the season in this shot, Moss following Fangio in their works Mercedes-Benz W196s, and learning every inch of the way. These were the definitively-styled slipper-bodied W196 Mercedes with exposed road wheels, but in truth Daimler-Benz's *Rennabteilung* was such a huge and well-funded undertaking that almost every race in which its Grand Prix cars appeared saw something new. Here Fangio is driving chassis '0013' and Moss '0012', both offering the Monaco-standard short wheelbase length of 2150 mm which meant there was no room ahead of the engine for the originally inboard front drum brakes which controlled the wheels through constant-velocity jointed shafts. Instead, in these cars the huge front drums were mounted outboard on the hubs. Moss's car here also featured a one-piece clamshell opening bonnet. They finished first and second, of course, but here for the first time it was Moss who finished in front.

British Grand Prix, Aintree – Very much the forgotten man, the German driver Karl Kling was a good, honest, very-hard trier who could never match the natural skill of his brilliant foreign team-mates despite self-confident assertions to the contrary. Sometimes his sheer determination to succeed took him off the road, but here at Liverpool he finished third in the latest chassis '0014' while Mercedes débutant Piero Taruffi completed Stuttgart's day in '0015', the team's four cars finishing 1-2-3-4. Ten years after the war had ended, this was *Deutschland über Alles* indeed.

1 October 1955 – Avon Trophy, Castle Combe – In minor British Formula 1 races the new Vanwall team really found its feet during this season. Here in sunny Wiltshire the Franco-American driver Harry Schell stormed to victory in Vanwall 'VW2', its original *Special* tag having been long-since dropped as the 4-cylinder Norton and Rolls-Royce influenced engine had grown to a full 2½-litres. It was powerful and relatively reliable, but the original Cooper-designed multi-tubular chassis was beginning to reveal its limitations. It is noticeable here, however, that the Vanwall toolroom was already manufacturing such items as the front suspension parts. Look at those lovely Ferrari-inspired wishbones, machined all over, where Cooper would have used simple bent and welded tube. These Vanwalls still relied heavily upon Ferrari practice, their rear-mounted transaxle gearbox was virtually a Chinese copy, and riveted fuel tanks, Borrani wire-spoked wheels, steering rack etc. were all very much Ferrari-style. The American Goodyear-patent ventilated disc brakes, however were borrowed from aeronautical practice and were unique to Vanwall in Formula 1. They became a powerful factor in the team's eventual success.

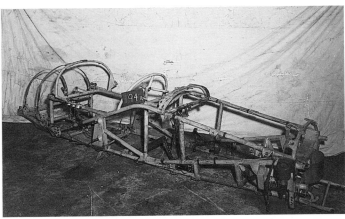

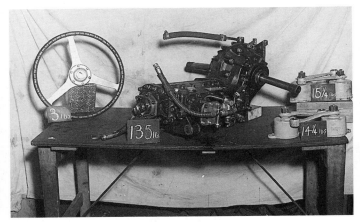

November, 1955 – Vandervell Products' racing shop, Acton, West London – Tony Vandervell appreciated his team needed a new chassis for 1956 and when Colin Chapman of Lotus was approached as chassis designer, what became the World Championship-winning series of teardrop Vanwalls was born – Chapman calling in his aerodynamicist associate Frank Costin to design the new body shape. As a baseline, the Castle Combe-winning car – chassis 'VW2' – was stripped and its major components weighed. Just for the record, they were photographed, as here; the Cooper-designed chassis scaled 194 lbs, the Ferrari-derived transaxle gearbox 135 lbs, the Ferrari-like Houdaille friction dampers 29½lbs and the steering wheel 3lbs. Vanwall would do better.

24 September 1955 – Gold Cup, Oulton Park – Following Lancia's mid-season collapse and absorption by Fiat, its racing team's hardware and designs were ceded to Ferrari. After an abortive attempt to campaign the existing D50s at Monza, the Scuderia eventually entered two in this minor British non-Championship race. Here is Mike Hawthorn driving the car which he qualified on pole position during practice, 0.2 sec faster than Moss's ultimately victorious Maserati. Hawthorn finished second and his team-mate Castellotti seventh after a delayed and troubled run. Virtually the only thing Ferrari about this Lancia is the yellow-and-black *Cavallino Rampante* shield upon its scuttle and the Englebert, instead of Pirelli, tyres. They certainly did not help.

Below left: September, 1955 – Testing at Monza about the time of the Italian Grand Prix – the latest Ferrari 555 *Super Squalo*, four of which ran in the race, driven by Castellotti, Hawthorn, Trintignant and Maglioli, finishing third, retiring, eighth and sixth respectively, were no match at all for the all-conquering Mercedes. Behind this 555 are technical manager Luigi Bazzi, 'Nino' Farina, chief mechanic Luigi Parenti and, in the white shirt, team manager Amarotti. The 555-specification, 4-cylinder engine had a wide 90 degree valve-angle head which lowered its overall height, permitting the flatter body profile used.

1956

FANGIO'S FERRARI FORTUNE...

Ferrari won a great prize by signing-up Fangio to drive for them following Mercedes' retirement while Stirling Moss returned to Maserati, which he had left for Mercedes in 1955. The fuel-injected Vanwall 4-cylinder engine was now punching out around 290bhp, matching Mercedes' 1955 figures, but just too late and still lacking a driver capable of winning with it. Tony Vandervell signed up Mike Hawthorn and Harry Schell while Moss had a one-off drive in the latest Colin Chapman-chassised, Frank Costin-bodied, teardrop Vanwall upon its début in the BRDC International Trophy at Silverstone, winning this short race handsomely. He was impressed by the car's speed and power, less so by its driveability and handling.

BRM signed Tony Brooks when free and Hawthorn, who in 1955 had reached an agreement with Vandervell that did not endure. However, the find of this season was Peter Collins, the former 500cc Formula 3 star who had driven for BRM and now joined Ferrari as understudy to Fangio and Castellotti. He promptly won the Belgian Grand Prix at Spa and the French race at Reims-Gueux, where Harry Schell gave Ferrari's complacent team's tail a terrific tweak with the Vanwalls, racing amongst them wheel-to-wheel until his own car gave trouble, whereupon he took over Hawthorn's sister car to occupy second place until the still inevitable problem struck it down. Moss and Brooks took note.

The new rear-engined Bugatti 251 appeared there, depressingly slow and uncompetitive perhaps because of, rather than in spite of Gioachino Colombo's startling transverse-mid-engined low polar moment of inertia design.

Through the speed trap on Silverstone's Hangar Straight during the British Grand Prix, Hawthorn's BRM P25 clocked 137.4mph, Schell's Vanwall 136.9, Brooks' ill-fated BRM 136.4, Fangio's Lancia-Ferrari 134.8 and Moss's Maserati 133.8mph.

Fangio won there and also in the German Grand Prix at the Nürburgring, where he averaged 3mph more than he had in the Mercedes-Benz W196 the previous year. At Monza the Italian Grand Prix again decided the Drivers' Championship – in Fangio's favour for the fourth time – but only after Schell's Vanwall had led on six occasions before it broke. Moss and Fangio had duelled until the Argentinian's rear suspension failed on the rough bankings, Collins – Fangio's only remaining rival for the Drivers' title – stopped from second place and handed his car to The Old Man. Moss won for Maserati with Fangio a delighted and relieved second, and again Champion of the World. Ron Flockhart finished third in his Connaught.

The top six placings in the 1956 World Championship of Drivers were:

Fangio (Lancia-Ferrari), World Champion Driver, with 30 points
Moss (Maserati), 2nd, with 27 points
Collins (Ferrari and Lancia-Ferrari), 3rd, with 25 points
Behra (Maserati), 4th, with 22 points
Castellotti (Lancia-Ferrari), 5th*, with 7½ points
Paul Frère (Lancia-Ferrari), 6th*, with 6 points.

Officially, Indianapolis '500' winner Pat Flaherty occupied sixth place with 8 World Championship points while Indy second-place man Sam Hanks was seventh-equal with Frère on six points. I have ignored these Indy drivers here to present the true road-racing Formula 1 picture.

There were only ten non-Championship races since so many of Europe's formerly ubiquitous minor public road circuits had closed in the backwash of the Le Mans disaster. Fangio's Lancia-Ferrari – of course – won the Buenos Aires City Grand Prix following the Argentine Championship round, and at Syracuse. Maserati won at Goodwood and Aintree (in the '200' driven by Moss, the '100' by privateer Horace Gould), at Snetterton (Salvadori) and in the Caen GP (Schell). The new Vanwall notched a Moss-driven début victory at Silverstone, and Gordini (Manzon) won at Naples.

Connaught salvaged a minor success at Brands Hatch (Archie Scott-Brown) – this great pioneering marque by this time on its last legs.

THE CARS COMPETING – 1956

BRM P25; Connaught A-Type and B-Type; Cooper-Bristol and Cooper-Aston Martin; Emeryson-Alta; Ferrari 555, 625 (and Lancia-Ferrari variants); Gordini *Types* 16 6-cyl and 32/32B 8-cyl; HWM; Lancia D50; Maserati 250F and A6GCM/250; Vanwall.

5 May 1956 – BRDC International Trophy, Silverstone – Britain's new white hope, the latest Peter Berthon and Stewart Tresilian-conceived 2½-litre BRM P25 pitches under braking with the tall – and apprehensive? – Mike Hawthorn, bow-tied, green-helmeted and green wind-cheatered, looming from its closely confined cockpit. The well-made P25 showed all BRM's familiar characteristics of admirable execution but disorganised preparation of an imperfect concept. The Project 25 designation really applied to the 2½-litre 4-cylinder engine, the relevant chassis being known strictly as the P27. The engine combined relatively short stroke and massively wide bore with a twin-camshaft wide-angle head design using hemispherical combustion chambers and two immense valves, which created equally immense problems. Tresilian was a brilliant consultant engineer whose original design had specified four smaller valves per cylinder, two exhaust and two inlets. When Connaught could not afford to adopt it, BRM took it on, but chief engineer Berthon felt BRM's development capability could not make the 4vpc idea raceworthy. The car's original big-tube chassis was light and simple, stiffened by the stress-skin semi-monocoque panelling visible here. Note the Dunlop alloy disc wheels in place of traditional Rudge-Whitworth wires. The car featured three disc brakes – outboard on the hubs up front, with a single rear disc on the back of the transaxle, cooled by the duct visible here behind Hawthorn's elbow. After narrowly escaping decapitation when the unsecured bonnet blew off during practice, he qualified 4th, 1 sec off Moss's Vanwall pole-time, but retired with timing gear failure after sharing fastest lap with Stirling, at 1:43.0, 102.30mph.

2 April 1956 – Glover Trophy, Goodwood, Easter Monday – The Connaught B-Type had first appeared in streamlined body form in the 1955 British Grand Prix at Aintree, but the one-piece body top's vulnerability and inconvenience in transit and in the pits and paddock led to rapid redesign. The B-Type as then rebodied in open-wheeled, slipper-body form by the little Send factory remained a sleek, well-balanced and very handsome car. Les Leston, driving chassis 'B6' here, finished third behind the Maserati 250Fs of Moss and Salvadori. Tony Brooks had driven a similar sister 'B1', to beat a strong Maserati field in the 1955 Syracuse Grand Prix. He and Connaught thus became the first all-British winner of a Continental Grand Prix Formula event since Segrave's Sunbeam won at San Sebastian in 1924, 31 years previously. Like the new BRM P25, the Connaught used Dunlop disc wheels. The body fit and finish, and general preparation look superb. Colour is British Racing Green with a contrasting recognition triangle atop the nose.

21 April 1956 – Aintree '200' – British streamliner; Connaught's B-Type had been introduced in 1955 with all-enveloping, centre seat bodywork like this. The elegant one-piece top proved, however, very vulnerable to costly and time-consuming damage from even an otherwise inconsequential bump. The theoretical advantage of improved straight line speed could not be exploited on the majority of circuits then in use. Here Desmond Titterington is driving chassis 'B5' at Aintree on the streamlined bodyshell's final appearance. The car's brakes gave trouble and the Ulsterman retired after 53 of 67 laps.

30 June 1956 – *Grand Prix de l'ACF* practice, Reims-Gueux – By this time the continually updated and developed Maserati 250Fs were wearing much smoother, smaller, unlouvred bodies compared with the early numbers' original 1954 style. Here, two of the private owner-drivers are seen at Thillois Corner; Louis Rosier clipping the apex in his French-blue car '2506', having just dived inside the Spaniard Francisco 'Paco' Godia-Sales's '2524'. Rosier finished sixth in the Grand Prix, three laps behind Peter Collins' winning Lancia-Ferrari while Godia encountered mechanical problems in this session and was unable to start on race day.

1 July 1956 – *Grand Prix de l'ACF*, Reims-Gueux – Battle Royal, and the emergence of a new name as Harry Schell's lofty teardrop Vanwall, chassis 'VW2', rushes up the inside under heavy braking at the end of the Soissons straight, lining up for the tight right-hander at Thillois, to the extreme discomfiture of the works Lancia-Ferrari D50As – Fangio leading from Castellotti and eventual winner Peter Collins. A Gordini holds a watching brief, behind. The Lancia-derived V8 Ferraris were fast but known as rather unwieldly, ill-handling cars (although Fangio disagrees) and now for the first time the Vanwall was proving its extreme straight-line speed and power. As yet all it lacked was reliability and a really top-flight driver to exploit it.

Below: Grand Prix de l'ACF, Reims-Gueux – The high-speed nature of the triangular public road circuit at Reims made it very attractive for those designers willing to risk trying their hand at producing an effective aerodynamic bodyshell. Few got it right – Daimler-Benz of course doing best with their well-researched and wind tunnel-tested *Stromlinienwagen* of 1954. They would

have returned with closed-wheelers in 1955 but the French race that year was cancelled following the Le Mans disaster. Here in 1956, Ferrari tested this nose fairing to make the most of the D50A shape with its inter-wheel sponsons, but their sums were wrong and the new nose lifted sharply at high speed, lightening the steering and allowing the car to dart and wander "even more than usual". Similar problems afflicted the Maserati, Vanwall and Cooper streamliners also tried at Reims.

Grand Prix de l'ACF, Reims-Gueux – Lancia-Ferrari unclothed in the team's Reims garage, clearly revealing how the pannier fuel tankage in these merged-body D50A cars enclosed the alcohol load further inboard than had their true Lancia D50 predecessors in separate outrigger tanks. This shot also reveals the massive rear-mounted combined gearbox and final-drive unit, here with half-shafts disconnected, the weighty tubular chassis frame members, rear de Dion tube running through the frame to link those finned drum brakes and hubs, lever-arm rear Houdaille friction dampers attached to the extreme lower-rear frame corners, and gaping pipework awaiting the removed tail fuel and oil tanks' return.

Opposite top: 14 July 1956 – British Grand Prix, Silverstone – Italian armoury; the Scuderia Ferrari line-up here in the paddock behind the pits in Northamptonshire, there being five D50As present, Olivier Gendebien's fifth-string car to the fore. Ferrari's experience with the original Lancia D50s when ceded them before the Italian 1955 Grand Prix had been that although the Vittorio Jano-designed cars' ultimate cornering power was certainly very high, their centralized mass concentration and consequent low polar moment of inertia made them too nervous to handle, insensitive near the ultimate limit of adhesion. To provide more 'feel' Ferrari progressively moved fuel capacity from the side tanks to the tail; the side sponsons by this time merely housing subsidiary tanks, albeit still quite capacious ones, and fairing-in the four-pipe exhaust runs each side. Note the Englebert tyres, and the Scuderia's OM transporter in the background; blue and yellow, the civic colours of Modena.

Right: British Grand Prix, Silverstone – Peter Collins driving an earlier-style Lancia-Ferrari without the merged-in side tank sponsons of the definitive 1957-style D50As. The separation of these sponsons, outrigged each side of the central fuselage, is clearly visible here, as is the severe understeer from which these heavy though powerful cars perpetually suffered. Even so, they were sufficiently effective for Fangio to win both this race, and his fourth World Championship title. He quite liked them.

104

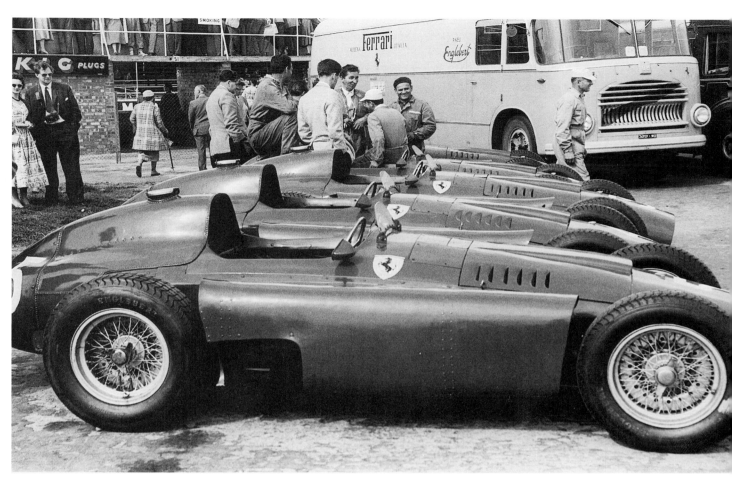

1957
MASERATI STEMS THE TIDE

This season was Fangio's last in full-time competition, for which he returned to Maserati who were his second love after the long-gone Alfa Corse team. For Fangio, Maserati built the ultimate *Tipo* 2 'Lightweight' 250F and teamed him with Jean Behra and Harry Schell. Ferrari, meanwhile, reunited Hawthorn and Collins within his team, joining Castellotti and Luigi Musso, who had abandoned Maserati with whom he had grown up in racing.

However, the British Vanwall was at last coming on strong, and Tony Vandervell's team could now combine really competitive horsepower, straightline speed and stable handling with adequate reliability and the strongest all-round driver team in the business: Stirling Moss, Tony Brooks, and the mercurial newcomer Stuart Lewis-Evans.

Eight World Championship rounds were run after the Dutch and Belgian Grands Prix had both been cancelled. Fangio and Maserati won the Argentinian, Monaco, French and German races; Moss and Brooks shared a Vanwall to win the British Grand Prix at Aintree, becoming the first British combination to win a *Grande Épreuve* since Segrave's Sunbeam at Tours in the 1923 *Grand Prix de l'ACF*. Moss followed up this literally breakthrough success with two crushing victories over the Italian cars on Italian soil, at Pescara, and in the Italian Grand Prix itself at Monza. These great successes were thoroughly relished by Tony Vandervell, his team and the British motor racing public in general. The final event of the year was the revived Moroccan Grand Prix at Casablanca, a non-Championship round, which fell to Behra's Maserati from Lewis-Evans' Vanwall.

Highlight of the season overall was perhaps the German Grand Prix in which Vanwall flopped badly as their cars refused to handle on the undulating and bumpy Nürburgring. This left Maserati and Ferrari to fight it out. Fangio had started with half-full tanks to build up sufficient time-cushion for a midway refuelling stop. Hawthorn and Collins pursued him ferociously in their latest Lancia-Ferrari 801s. Unfortunately, Fangio's pit stop was then botched and by the time he had rejoined the fray Hawthorn and Collins were long gone. The stage was set.

From third place Fangio turned on one of the greatest come-back drives in racing history. After bedding in his fresh tyres he threw all caution to the winds and exploited to the full all his peerless single-seater skill, experience and judgement. He simply pulverized the lap record, lap after lap. He didn't just catch the two talented and rapid young Englishmen in their powerful Ferraris. As one reporter put it, "He simply ate them alive". With a lap to go he passed first Collins, then Hawthorn, to win by 3.6 secs at a record average of over 88 mph for the 312 miles. With this great victory, Fangio clinched his fifth and final World Championship title with the finest drive of a glittering career. Neither Hawthorn nor Collins begrudged him such success: "How can you live with the Old Man when he's in that kind of mood . . ." they laughed.

BRM claimed only a third place at Casablanca but Jean Behra had previously scored their first-ever Formula 1 win in the non-Championship Caen Grand Prix, and in the similar-level International Trophy late that year at Silverstone the BRM team's P25s finished 1-2-3. There were eight other non-Championship races, of which Maserati won half; at Buenos Aires (Fangio) and at Pau, Modena and Casablanca (all Behra). Lancia-Ferrari won at Syracuse and Naples (both Collins) and at Reims (Musso), while Connaught won the less important Glover Trophy at Goodwood (Lewis-Evans).

The 1957 World Championship of Drivers table ended as follows:

Fangio (Maserati), World Champion Driver, with 40 points
Moss (Maserati and Vanwall), 2nd, with 25 points
Musso (Lancia-Ferrari), 3rd, with 16 points
Hawthorn (Lancia-Ferrari), 4th, with 13 points
Brooks (Vanwall), 5th, with 11 points
Gregory (Maserati), 6th, with 10 points

Meanwhile, a new 1½-litre Formula 2 had been officially introduced this season – after a number of British dress-rehearsal events in 1956 – as a rung on the ladder towards Formula 1.

It was a pump-fuel Formula, its regulations demanding true gasoline as opposed to the witches' brew alcohol fuels universal in Formula 1. Pressure by the fuel companies had been increasing for some time to change Formula 1 to an Aviation Spirit or 'AvGas' class, as this would enable them to promote their own pump fuel brands relevant to Grand Prix success. The CSI announced that the extension of the 2½-litre Formula from 1958 to the end of 1960 was going to incorporate this change, and there was more. The most significant new measure, apart from the new AvGas-only rule which would improve fuel consumption was that minimum World Championship Grand Prix distance was to be reduced from 500kms (312mls) or three hours, to 300kms (180mls) or two hours. AvGas would reduce maximum engine power, but crucially the better consumption it offered would also enable cars to carry smaller fuel tanks. Add to this the shorter Grand Prix distances now required and this enabled fuel capacity on board the cars to be reduced even further, thus prompting the design of smaller, less bulky cars than ever before.

This move for 1958, allied to the 1957 introduction of International Formula 2 as a pump-fuel class, prompted development of an interesting new breed of car. It would quickly topple the established régime.

Cooper had begun to build tiny little rear-engined Formula 2 cars using proprietary 4-cylinder pump-fuel engines built by Coventry Climax. Lotus had begun to build skinny little front-engined Formula 2 cars, their Type 12s, using similar engines of c.140bhp. Ferrari viewed Formula 2 as another money-earning opportunity and developed a new 1500cc Dino V6 engine whose c.170hp could eat the Climax for breakfast. This new Italian engine was installed in a 'smallish' front-engined traditional chassis and as a works Formula 2 car it could destroy Cooper's hopes and those of the less reliable and not quite so nimble Lotus on fast circuits. By the end of that 1957 season, Enzo Ferrari had decided that this Dino V6 engine should be progressively enlarged towards a 2½-litre Formula 1 capacity for 1958. Interim-sized V6 Ferrari Dinos burning AvGas competed in both the Modena and Casablanca Grands Prix at the end of that season and excelled. The por-

tents were good for 1958 – the stage seemingly set for a battle royal between Ferrari, Maserati, BRM and Vanwall.

The Front-Engined Cars Competing – 1957

Alfa Romeo *Speciale*; BRM P25; Connaught B-Type; Emeryson-Alta; Ferrari *Tipo* 801, Dino 156 F2 and interim F1 models, 625, (and Lancia-Ferrari variants); Gordini Type 16 and 32; HWM; Lancia-Marino *Speciale*; Lancia-Ferrari D50A; Lister-Climax F2; Lotus-Climax Type 12 F2; Maserati 250F and A6G; OSCA; Vanwall.

Overleaf inset: 27 January 1957 – Buenos Aires City Grand Prix, Argentina – The non-Championship race following the Argentine Grand Prix which Fangio won for Maserati, saw Peter Collins win Heat Two in Luigi Musso's D50A. Here the young Englishman is cornering at high speed, just fending off the attentions of Harry Schell's works Maserati 250F '2511'.

Overleaf main picture: March, 1957 – Team Lotus test day, Silverstone – While the great Grand Prix teams of Ferrari, Maserati, Vanwall and BRM were preparing their latest wares for the new European season, and the unfortunate, under-financed Connaught company, abandoned by its long-time sponsor Ken McAlpine, looked straight down the gunbarrel of impending closure, this little projectile was streaking round Silverstone. It is the prototype 1½-litre Formula 2 Lotus Type 12, Colin Chapman's first serious single-seat racing car design after the teardrop Vanwall. Ron Flockhart is testing it here, a tiny cigar of a car barely broader than its driving seat, no taller than the driver's shoulders; a minimalist approach in every way consistent with mounting a Coventry Climax FPF 4-cylinder engine ahead of the driver, i.e. needing a propeller-shaft to transmit drive past him (in this case below) to the rear axle. These cars would grow into 1.96 and then 2.2-litre form to compete in Formula 1 racing during 1958. Chapman and Team Lotus learned from them, and in 1960 would begin winning *Grandes Épreuves* at last, with the rear-engined Type 18.

April, 1957 – Another new Formula 2 car undergoing its initial shake-down tests, in this case the front-engined Ferrari Dino 156 with Jano-designed 1500cc V6-cylinder 4-cam engine being driven by factory *collaudatore* Martino Severi on the public Maranello-Serramazzone road. The little car shows off its neat Scaglietti-built body in unpainted aluminium. It is badged as a Ferrari and beneath that scoop-topped bonnet the engine cam-covers carried '*Ferrari*' lettering; the familiar '*Dino*' script on these Formula 1 and 2 V6s would follow later. This is chassis '0011' and it would make its race début driven by Musso in the Naples Grand Prix on April 28 1957. It finished third there, won the Reims Formula 2 *Coupe de Vitesse* in July driven by Trintignant and at the end of the season was uprated to interim Formula 1 form with an 1893cc engine matching that of its new sister, '0012'. In these two AvGas (as opposed to alcohol)-burning cars Musso and Collins finished second and third in the Modena Grand Prix. For the Moroccan race closing the season at Casablanca, '0012' in full Dino 246 F1 engine trim was driven by Collins, and '0011' with a further-enlarged 2195cc engine by Hawthorn. Neither finished, but the Ferrari Dino Formula 1 line had been founded.

Opposite top: 18 July 1957 – First day's practice for the British Grand Prix, Aintree. A splendid sight, the works Vanwall team's four gleaming, toolroom-built genuine Grand Prix cars arrayed in echelon before the Aintree pits in preparation for the first *Grande Épreuve* they would actually win. No 20, chassis 'VW4' with engine 'V4' started the race driven by Tony Brooks, and finished it in first place after having been taken over by Stirling Moss. No 22, chassis 'VW5' with engine 'V2' ran second driven by Stuart Lewis-Evans until its throttle linkage disintegrated, the brilliant but frail young Londoner eventually placing seventh, but disqualified for abandoning its bonnet on-circuit. Number 18, chassis 'VW1', engine 'V3', led the race early on driven by Moss until its engine faltered, Brooks taking it over after handing his original race car to Moss, but the magneto failed before the finish.

Right: British Grand Prix, Aintree – The soaring moment as Stirling Moss acknowledges the chequered flag in Vanwall 'VW4', the car in which Tony Brooks, still suffering the after-effects of his heavy shunt at Le Mans in an Aston Martin, had started the race – after Moss's own had struck trouble. As the Vanwall won, at long last achieving Tony Vandervell's great ambition of beating "those bloody red cars", a new era of motor racing history dawned. After being quickly put in their place by an appalling showing at Nürburgring in the German Grand Prix, Vanwall beat the Maseratis and Ferraris twice more, this time on their home soil in Italy, at both Pescara and Monza. The balance was shifting, but Ferrari would stage a fierce rearguard action for the old Establishment throughout 1958.

British Grand Prix, Aintree – Jean Behra demonstrating the peerless lines of the quintessential front-engined Italian Grand Prix car, the *Tipo* 2 or 'Lightweight' Maserati 250F of which just three were built purely for the works team that season. These cars used smaller-gauge chassis tubing than their works and customer-series predecessors, although the 'Lightweight' tag was of course a relative term. The trio's chassis numbers were '2527', '28' and '29', Behra's mount here being '2528' whose clutch burst on lap 69, scattering debris which burst a tyre on Hawthorn's Ferrari and enabled Moss to retake the lead for Vanwall. Driving the sister car '2529', Fangio staged his magnificent drives in this, his final full season of racing, to win both French and German Grands Prix. The latter event was an all-time classic as he lost much time in a bungled mid-race refuelling stop, was left well astern by Hawthorn and Collins's leading Ferraris, and then in a tigerish comeback drive "simply ate them alive", to win again and clinch his fifth and final Drivers World Championship title.

18 August 1957 – *Gran Premio Pescara*, Italy – For the first and only time the 27 km (17 ml) Pescara circuit on the Adriatic coast hosted a World Championship-qualifying Formula 1 race. Here under the grilling sun Stirling Moss leads in his winning Vanwall, chassis 'VW5' with engine 'V4', setting a new lap record on the way. Vanwall confronted a full team from Maserati, for whom Fangio qualified on pole but could only finish second, while Ferrari sent a solitary Lancia-Ferrari 801, seen in the background here, for Luigi Musso, who retired when the rough course shook his oil tank loose. Second blood to the Vanwalls and on Italian soil too. They would go one better yet, and win again at Monza after qualifying 1-2-3 on the starting grid.

1958

THE WIND OF CHANGE...

While Ferrari forethought – as usual – meant the Italian team had made a head start for the revised new Formula, other teams, particularly Vanwall and BRM, made tardy progress towards converting their existing 4-cylinder engines to run effectively on AvGas in place of alcohol fuels. When the Argentine Grand Prix was organized at very short notice to open this new season, both British teams bleated at its inclusion in the world Championship. When

Stirling Moss went there and beat Ferrari in the Rob Walker team's tiny little Formula 2-based interim Cooper-Climax not only the crowd was incredulous. So were Ferrari, and the other British teams which had not made the trip, Moss, the Walker team and Cooper Cars in particular! Both Vanwall and BRM immediately dropped protests already entered with the FIA on the Argentine event's late inclusion in the calendar.

Second round of the Championship was at Monaco, where Walker's other driver Maurice Trintignant won in a sister interim Cooper using a slightly larger 2070cc Climax engine in a similar rear-engined Formula 2-derived chassis. Thereafter, Vanwall got into its stride with Moss and Brooks who respectively won the Dutch, Portuguese and Moroccan, Belgian, German and Italian Grands Prix. Ferrari's team of Dino 246 V6 cars was led by Hawthorn with Collins and Musso as his main support. Hawthorn won the French Grand Prix on sheer speed and power but the hapless Musso tried too hard on that narrow and unforgiving circuit and was killed. Two weeks later Peter Collins led Hawthorn home 1-2 in the British Grand Prix at Silverstone but two weeks after that great win, Collins was killed at the Nürburgring while attempting to catch Brooks' Vanwall for the lead.

Hawthorn was left an embittered and grieving man. He drove on towards the end of the season which he had decided would be his last. Whatever the outcome of the Championship he had decided to retire. However, he still drove hard enough to set a string of fastest race laps, each of which secured for him an extra Championship point. When Moss won the deciding Moroccan Grand Prix at Casablanca and set fastest lap for Vanwall he could have done no more, yet it was not enough. Hawthorn trailed his wheel-tracks to the line to finish second and steal the World Championship of Drivers' title by just one solitary point. After so many years as perennial runner-up the title perhaps should have gone to Moss, but instead it was Hawthorn who became the first-ever British World Champion Driver. Stirling would never win the crown even though he was every inch Fangio's natural successor as the standard-setter of his day. Mike Hawthorn was thus World Champion and he retired from racing to concentrate upon his business interests, but in January 1959 was killed in a road accident near home.

Vanwall also won that year the inaugural Formula 1 Constructors' World Championship which had been instituted that season. This defeat of Ferrari at last brought recognition to British motor racing efforts which had been gathering pace and influence ever since the end of World War 2. The balance of power in top-level motor racing was changing fast. For years British drivers had shown true World class but there had been a dearth of British cars good enough to carry them. Now with Vanwall leading the way, the era of British Grand Prix domi-

nation was about to dawn. The French had had their day, so had the Germans and Italians. Now it would be the green cars' turn – but for our story here, their engines would be in the wrong end . . .

The 1958 World Championship of Drivers had been the closest yet, and its final result was:

Hawthorn (Ferrari), World champion Driver, with 42 points
Moss (Vanwall), 2nd, with 41 points
Brooks (Vanwall), 3rd, with 24 points
Salvadori (Cooper-Climax rear-engined), 4th, with 15 points
Collins (Ferrari), 5th equal, with 14 points*
Schell (Maserati and BRM), 5th equal, with 14 points
*Crashed fatally during season.

There were only five non-Championship Formula 1 events; Ferrari winning the Glover Trophy at Goodwood (Hawthorn), the International Trophy at Silverstone (Collins), and the Syracuse Grand Prix (Musso). Most significantly, the other two minor races both fell to Stirling Moss – driving a rear-engined Walker Cooper.

The Front-Engined Cars Competing – 1958

BRM P25; Connaught B-Type; Emeryson-Alta; Ferrari Dino 246 and 156 F2; Lotus-Climax Types 12 and 16 F1 and F2; Maserati 250F; OSCA; Vanwall.

Main picture: 19 January 1958 – Argentine Grand Prix, Buenos Aires – Virus in the system as Stirling Moss's tiny 1.96-litre Cooper-Climax entered by private owner Rob Walker is about to achieve the first postwar *Grande Épreuve* victory scored by a car carrying its engine behind its driver. It was nothing more than an over-engined Formula 2 special and Stirling achieved this historic feat by running non-stop, nursing Continental tyres which were worn through to the canvas at the finish. The new works Ferrari Dino 246s were much faster, but the team failed to recognise the Moss/Walker tactics until too late. Here Stirling signals Bristolian garage owner Horace Gould aside in his slow private Maserati '2514' while Godia's sister '2524' (8) has already been successfully lapped and Hawthorn's Dino 246 is fast approaching the braking area in frantic but belated pursuit.

Inset: 26 May 1958 – Dutch Grand Prix, Zandvoort – Third round of the first World Championship season to be run to the new AvGas-burning Formula, with its shortened race requirement, became the first of the year's *Grandes Épreuves* to be won by a traditional front-engined Grand Prix car! Neither Vanwall nor BRM had been ready to contest the opening Argentine Grand Prix, hastily organised at short notice that January, and Moss drove Walker's tiny Cooper there "more or less for fun". After its unexpected win, round two at Monaco fell to Maurice Trintignant's 2.1-litre Walker Cooper, but here on the more open Dutch seaside course the sheer power of the front-engined cars left the more nimble small-engined Coopers gasping. Moss had resumed his Vanwall contract, and here he is in the graceful 'VW10', set for victory. The Acton team had planned to fit those new cast 'wobbly-web' pattern wheels all round, but in testing the drivers preferred the extra steering 'give' and 'feel' provided by the Borrani wire-spoked type up front.

Dutch Grand Prix, Zandvoort – Hawthorn's Ferrari Dino 246 had been refined for 1958 into a compact, neat but fierce little V6 car with abundant power and rather demanding handling. It also suffered from Ferrari's insistence upon running on inadequate Belgian Englebert racing tyres, which were no match for the new technology Dunlop Racing covers then in use by Vanwall and BRM. One of the Bourne team's 4-cylinder P25s driven by Jean Behra is dogging Hawthorn's wheel-tracks here; the two light, very powerful and well-faired P25s driven by the Frenchman and his team-mate Harry Schell eventually finishing second and third here behind Moss's Vanwall. At last the much-maligned BRM had demonstrated real reliability, although these Grands Prix were shorter than ever before...

Opposite top: 15 June 1958 – Belgian Grand Prix, Spa-Francorchamps – Vanwalls were again in rampant form at Spa where Tony Brooks won in 'VW5' but Moss missed a gear and blew-up 'VW10' while leading on the opening lap. Lewis-Evans here in 'VW4' finished third behind Hawthorn's Ferrari Dino after a collision at this very spot (La Source hairpin) with Gendebien's factory Dino. On this superfast, curving and undulating course Lewis-Evans preferred the new cast wheels front and rear. Note his car's exhaust system, lost in the body cutout provided for the earlier 'four-finger' manifolding of 1957.

Right: 5 July 1958 – Team Lotus garage before the *Grand Prix de l'ACF*, Reims-Gueux – The first of the last group of front-engined Grand Prix Lotuses was being prepared by Jim Endruweit for Graham Hill to drive in the *Grande Épreuve* next day. This was the Type 16, with Vanwall-style teardrop body, Coventry Climax FPF 4-cylinder engine laid over to the offside at 62 degrees from vertical and offset 5½ degrees from the chassis centreline to spear its prop-shaft to the left of the driver's seat, powering Lotus's latest positive-stop five-speed 'queerbox' transmission. This layout provided a very low if broad body cross-section, but the engine thoroughly objected to lying on its ear and lubrication and scavenging problems created power loss to add to that already absorbed by the angled propeller shaft's multiple joints. Yet the Mercedes-Benz W196 featured 'lay-down' engine mounting, as did many Offy roadsters at Indianapolis. Even so, Chapman heeded Climax's predictions of doom and the sister Formula 2 Type 16 which also débuted at Reims had its FPF engine mounted more upright, canted 17 degrees to the nearside. Team Lotus would find a simpler way for 1960, but it took them all of 1959 to conclude that the front-engined configuration – even that of the advanced Type 16 – was outmoded.

Main picture: 6 July 1958 – *Grand Prix de l'ACF*, Reims-Gueux – Sign of the times; in 1953 Mike Hawthorn's Ferrari had narrowly beaten Juan Fangio's Maserati to the line to win the French Grand Prix. Here on the same circuit five years later, Fangio is driving his works-entered *Piccolo* Maserati 250F '2533' in his last motor race, and although Hawthorn will win again for Ferrari the *Maestro* has three British cars breathing down his neck, and preparing to pass him. They are Moss's Vanwall 'VW10' (8), and the BRM P25s of Schell (16) and Behra (14). While JMF finished fourth, Moss was second and the BRMs, after mid-race problems, finished unclassified eleventh and twelfth.

Inset: 19 October 1958 – Moroccan Grand Prix, Ain-Diab public road circuit, Casablanca – Mike Hawthorn has featured prominently in this account since 1952. Here he is pictured driving his faithful Ferrari Dino 246, now converted to disc brakes, for the last time and in his last motor race, heading towards second place behind Moss in the Grand Prix but to victory by one point in that season's World Championship of Drivers. He thus became the first British driver to achieve that honour, and as the age of the front-engined Grand Prix car approached its own passing it was the new British marques like Cooper and Lotus which would set the future pace.

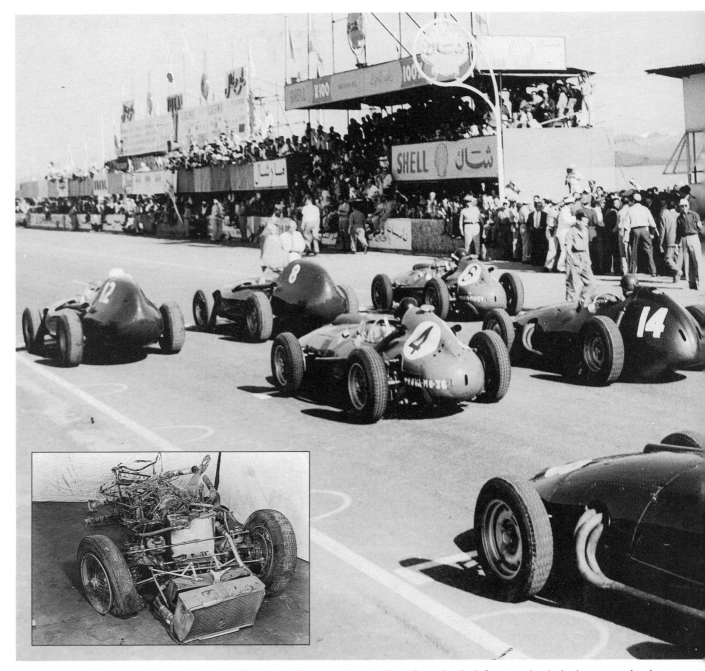

Main picture: Moroccan Grand Prix, Ain-Diab, Casablanca – For the last time classical front-engined single-seaters dominate the head of the starting grid for a World-Championship-qualifying Grand Prix. Nearest the camera here on the third row are Jo Bonnier's BRM P25 (18), Tony Brooks' Vanwall (10), Olivier Gendebien's Ferrari Dino 246 (2); ahead on the second row are Phil Hill's Ferrari (4) and Jean Behra's BRM P25 (14), and on the front row the Vanwalls of Lewis-Evans (12) and Moss (8), with of course Hawthorn's Ferrari Dino 246 on pole; an historic scene, never to be repeated.

Inset: October, 1958 – Vanwall racing shop, Acton, West London – All that remained of Vanwall 'VW4' after the engine seizure, spin and fire triggered by the fuel tank being burst against a roadside obstruction which fatally injured Stuart Lewis-Evans at Casablanca. This tragedy coupled to his own failing health and his doctors' insistence that he should slow down prompted Tony Vandervell to withdraw his magnificent team from serious competition. No competitive achievement could of course compensate for a lost life, but the reality of motor racing was that such things happen. Vanwall had just won the FIA's inaugural Formula 1 Constructors' World Championship title and in 1959-60 the rear-engined Coopers, which were in so many ways the complete antithesis of Vanwall's toolroom way of going racing, would defend it against those red Ferraris.

1 9 5 9
COOPER LEADS THE WAY

While Vanwall had secured the Formula 1 Constructor's World Championship title in that deciding race of 1958, they had also lost Stuart Lewis-Evans who crashed fatally. This tragedy, following the realisation of his long-

cherished ambition to "beat those bloody red cars" and the failure of his own health, persuaded Tony Vandervell to withdraw his great team from serious competition. Vanwalls would race again, but with no realistic prospect of proving either successful, or even competitive.

In the place of these exquisitely-built racing machines, the cheaper, simpler, 'blacksmithery' which was Cooper attained new heights. The 1959 season really witnessed the so-called 'Rear-

Engined Revolution' in Grand Prix car design.

Cooper led the way, now equipped with full 2½-litre Type FPF engines from Coventry Climax. With around 245 bhp and meaty mid-range torque these nimble and forgiving little cars enabled their Australian number one driver Jack Brabham to win the British and Monaco Grands Prix. Moss in Rob Walker's similar big-engined Cooper-Climax cars then won the Portuguese and Italian rounds while Cooper's number two driver Bruce McLaren emphasized the cars' true class by winning the inaugural United States Grand Prix at Sebring. That event rounded-off the season and saw Jack Brabham clinch at last his World Championship title to add to the Cooper Car Company's Constructors' Cup success.

Enzo Ferrari had signed-up Tony Brooks after Vanwall's withdrawal. Now this quiet but so immensely talented Englishman won for Ferrari in the French and German Grands Prix – the latter at the AVUS, in Berlin. Ferrari's new Dino V6 cars were immensely fast, but so were BRM's front-engined P25s in their latest guise. At last they won a Championship round as Jo Bonnier triumphed in the Dutch race at Zandvoort. Reliability was still the Bourne team's bugbear, as it was the Walker team's whose especially-made Italian gearboxes by Colotti (ex-Maserati) lost Moss at least two Grands Prix. Consequently Moss arranged to drive a BRM P25 in the French and British Grands Prix mid-season, the car being prepared by his father's British Racing Partnership team and sprayed a pale green. However, Stirling spun and stalled after losing the clutch in blazing heat at Reims, and was then delayed by a late stop to finish second at Aintree. He returned to the Walker Cooper, and its Colotti gearbox problems, thereafter and again narrowly missed the World title he so richly deserved.

This season also saw Aston Martin turning to Grand Prix racing at last, but its DBR4/250 car designed contemporarily with the 'Lightweight' series Maserati 250Fs of 1957 was too large, too late, and the effort behind it proved too little for success.

A more promising British newcomer was Colin Chapman's ultra-lightweight Lotus-Climax Type 16 whose only real problem, apart from structural frangibility, was that its engine was in

the front. By this time, that was clearly the wrong end. This would be corrected for 1960 from which point the Lotus legend would rapidly grow. By the end of 1959, BRM had already taken the tip from Cooper, and their rear-engined P48 prototype car made its first runs at Monza. BRM was back in the leading edge of Formula 1 technology now, after years in the wilderness and Ferrari, Lotus and the rest would follow them in Cooper's wake.

While Jack Brabham won the World Championship of Drivers' title by amassing 31 points in his rear-engined Cooper-Climax, the top six championship scores by drivers of front-engined cars were these:

Brooks (Ferrari), 2nd, with 27 points
Phil Hill (Ferrari), 4th, with 20 points
Dan Gurney (Ferrari), 7th, with 13 points
Bonnier (BRM), 8th, with 10 points
Ireland (Lotus-Climax), 12th equal, (F1 as opposed to Indy drivers), with 5 points
Schell (BRM, but also drove a Cooper-Climax), 12th equal with 5 points.

Stirling Moss, who finished 3rd overall in the Championship, had scored six of his 25½ points in the BRP-entered BRM P25, but the majority were scored in Rob Walker's rear-engined Cooper-Climax cars.

Again there were only five non-Championship Formula 1 events this season, of which Jean Behra won the Aintree '200' for Ferrari and Ron Flockhart the insignificant Silver City Trophy race for BRM at Snetterton. The other three events all fell – most significantly – to the rear-engined Coopers . . .

The Front-Engined Cars Competing – 1959

Aston Martin DBR4; BRM P25; Connaught C-Type; Cooper-Alta; Ferrari Dino 246 and 256, 156 F2; KurtisKraft-Offenhauser Midget; Lotus-Climax Type 16 and Type 12 F1 and F2; Maserati 250F; Vanwall.

Winter, 1958-9 – A beaming Jean Behra has just joined Ferrari from BRM and here at the Modena *Aerautodromo* he tries the latest Fantuzzi-bodied Dino 246 Formula 1 car for size, with chief engineer Carlo Chiti and Enzo Ferrari on the right. These cars used the latest version of the powerful 4-cam V6 Dino engine, plus Dunlop disc brakes and Dunlop Racing tyres as standard in place of the vilified old Ferrari drums and Englebert tyres of preceding seasons.

Overleaf: 2 May 1959 – BRDC International Trophy, Silverstone – A new heavyweight's first time in the ring looked quite promising as the long-awaited Aston Martin DBR4/250, originally conceived in parallel with the 'Lightweight' Maserati 250F of 1957, finally made its début. Roy Salvadori driving here had qualified this small-tube spaceframe, 6-cylinder dohc engined good-looker, third fastest behind Moss's borrowed BRM P25 and Brooks's latest Ferrari Dino 246. In this 235 km (146 ml) race he finished a good second behind Brabham's victorious now 2½-litre Cooper-Climax, even though when stripped, his engine bearings were found to be on their last legs, which boded ill for full-length Grands Prix. More promisingly, Salvadori had also set fastest race lap. However, from here on it was all downhill for Aston's Formula 1 ambitions, the design proving in effect too much, too late. See how it dwarfs Innes Ireland's pursuing Lotus 16.

Above: 31 May 1959 – Dutch Grand Prix, Zandvoort – This shot conveys a revealing direct comparison in simple size between the front-engined Lotus-Climax 16, a chronic understeerer you will notice, driven by Innes Ireland (12) and the rear-engined Walker Team Cooper-Climax Type 51 in his wheel tracks. There is really very little in it for height or width, but the Lotus is simply a longer, less functional machine. Ireland drove very well in this, his maiden *Grande Épreuve*, to finish a worthy fourth, while Trintignant was delayed to finish eighth. The winner after the Coopers of Moss and Brabham retired was Jo Bonnier's front-engined BRM. Bourne had won a *Grande Épreuve* after 10 seasons of endeavour.

5 July 1959 – *Grand Prix de l'ACF*, Reims-Gueux – The Empire strikes back as the elegant driving skills of former Vanwall team member Tony Brooks conduct his Ferrari Dino 256 through Thillois Corner. He is heading towards victory in the French Grand Prix, despite soaring mid-summer temperatures on the Champagne plain and the orange juice in the drinking bottle mounted within his cockpit reaching boiling point. These 1959-series Ferraris wore this more bulky body style by Fantuzzi since the team's normal competition coachbuilder, Scaglietti, was fully occupied at that time with production car work. Sadly for Tony Brooks, there was no Belgian Grand Prix that year at Spa, where he had won on every visit thus far whether he was driving sports or Grand Prix cars. He would narrowly miss the World Championship title for the second successive season, as would Moss for the fifth year running.

10 September 1959 – Pre-practice scene at Monza, prior to the Italian Grand Prix – Le Mans-winning driver Carroll Shelby's works Aston Martin DBR4/250 – chassis '2' – being fettled before the pits, showing off its Avon racing tyres (unique to the Feltham team), twin-plug ignition (count the plug leads), coil-and-wishbone independent front suspension and de Dion-axle rear end. An all-independent DBR5/250 model was developed rather half-heartedly for 1960, but it stood no chance against Cooper and Lotus designs with the engine in the right place – behind the driver.

1960

DEATH OF THE DINOSAURS

Jack Brabham and the latest 'Lowline' rear-engined Cooper-Climax dominated this season with five consecutive, mid-season Grand Prix victories. He and his team exerted a grip upon the class such as had not been seen since the days of Mercedes-Benz, the Ferrari 500s and the Alfa Romeo *Alfettas*.

However, at non-Championship level it was Colin Chapman's new rear-engined Lotus-Climax 18s which did the lion's share of winning. The only front-engined cars of any significance were the latest all-independently suspended Ferrari Dino 246/60s. They were driven most notably by team leader Phil Hill. In the meantime, the BRM P25s said farewell in Argentina and at Goodwood as the season began, the rear-engined P48s taking over thereafter for the bulk of this last year of the 2½-litre Formula.

The only other worthwhile front-engined cars to appear were Woolworth heir Lance Reventlow's long-awaited American team of Scarabs, and the Aston Martin in its latest lightened DBR5/250 form. Against Cooper and Lotus opposition, neither stood a chance. Both had lost too much time in the design office. Had they appeared in 1958 they might have shone. As it was against the latest in rear-engined opposition it was strictly no contest.

Only when the major British teams all boycotted the Italian Grand Prix – because the dangerous and bumpy combined road and high-speed banked track circuit was being used once more – was Ferrari able to win a Grand Prix, and by that time even they had a rear-engined prototype car out and racing. By the time of the United States Grand Prix at Riverside, California, which brought to a close seven seasons of 2½-litre Formula 1 racing, only Bob Drake's vintage Maserati 250F emerged as a finisher carrying engine ahead of driver. Maserati's 250F model thus achieved the unique distinction of having run in both the first and last events of this very important and at that time, longest-lived Formula.

Only five drivers of front-engined cars featured in the final results at the end of the 1960 World Championship of Drivers:

Phil Hill (Ferrari), 5th with 16 points (1 scored in a rear-engined Cooper-Climax in the US GP, closing race of the season which Ferrari had declined to enter)
Wolfgang von Trips (Ferrari), 7th, with 10 points
Richie Ginther (Ferrari), 8th F1 driver, with 8 points
Cliff Allison (Ferrari), 11th, with 6 points
Willy Mairesse (Ferrari), 13th equal, with 4 points

Amongst non-Championship Formula 1 races, of which there were yet again five, Lotus won four and Cooper one – with not even a front-engined front runner in sight – how times had changed.

The Front-Engined Cars Competing – 1960

Aston Martin DBR4/250 and DBR5/250; BRM P25; Cooper-Alta; Ferrari Dino 246/60; Lotus Type 16 and Type 12; Maserati 250F; Scarab; Vanwall.

18 May 1960 – Glover Trophy, Goodwood – At Acton, Vandervell Products had continued to toy with development of their one-time dominant World Championship-winning front-engined cars. Vanwall 'VW5' had been cut about and lowered and reappeared in the 1959 British Grand Prix at Aintree in a one-off outing driven by Tony Brooks on loan from Ferrari. It ran poorly and retired after only 14 laps with ignition trouble. For 1960 a more extensive, and expensive, final twitch of the old British giant produced a true 'Lowline' car for the French Grand Prix at Reims, but first, here in Sussex on Easter Monday, Tony Brooks had one last outing in 'VW5' in 'semi-Lowline' form, and running with cast wheels fore and aft. This graceful car was large, heavy and unwieldy compared to the new works 2½-litre Lotus 18s and Coopers with their Climax FPF engines, which Brooks had to chase. He finished seventh, his best practice lap of 1:26.8 having been no better than eighth fastest, two whole seconds slower than Chris Bristow's Yeoman Credit team Cooper-Climax on pole. Times had changed, very, very quickly and despite building one half-hearted rear-engined car, Vanwall had no place in this new era.

19 June 1960 – Belgian Grand Prix, Spa-Francorchamps – Phil Hill, Ferrari team leader, stamping hard on his latest all-independently suspended Ferrari Dino 246/60's disc brakes on the entry to La Source hairpin above the pits. His car here is chassis '0007' which still survives today, powered by a 3-litre Tasman V12 engine, in the good hands of English enthusiast and racer Neil Corner (who would himself win in the car at this venue in May 1991). On the superfast *Circuit Nationale*, Phil was able to unleash all Ferrari's *circa* 290 bhp at 8800 rpm and in a terrific practice effort he qualified on the front row of the starting grid and equalled the race fastest lap set by the otherwise uncatchable Jack Brabham's latest 'Lowline' Cooper-Climax T53. See here the more compact and graceful lines of these 1960 cars, the coil-spring/damper strut visible on the independent rear suspension, clear perspex carburettor cowl topping the bonnet, midships pannier tank section and disc brake visible in that right-front wire wheel.

Belgian Grand Prix, Spa-Francorchamps – American hopes for Woolworth heir Lance Reventlow's ambitious Scarab project foundered like Aston Martin's in too-lengthy development and an emergence on the European Grand Prix scene at least two seasons too late. The Scarab had been beautifully crafted in Venice, California by experienced sports-racing and hot-rod constructors, using a multi-tubular spaceframe in small-diameter lightweight stock and featuring all-independent suspension. Former pre-war Miller design engineer Leo Goossen played a major role in the Offenhauser-like dohc 4-cylinder engine which was canted steeply in the frame to provide that very low bonnet line. It used desmodromic valve gear and Hilborn fuel injection but despite making a fantastic noise it never provided the horsepower projected. Reventlow and Chuck Daigh drove two of these predominantly metallic mid-blue and white cars in the early-season European races but ran out of money and enthusiasm by the time of the French race at Reims, after which they returned home. One car later returned to run in English Intercontinental Formula events in 1961, using a 3-litre engine, but Daigh crashed it at Silverstone and that was the end. Three cars were built, the last never completed, followed by one blind alley rear-engined ICF version which raced briefly in Australian Tasman events. Here owner/constructor Reventlow has his baby sitting well down under full power, climbing the *Raidillon* curve after Eau Rouge. He qualified fifteenth and Daigh seventeenth on the Belgian Grand Prix grid, his best lap 19.7 secs slower than Brabham's Cooper on pole. His engine failed on lap one of the race, Daigh's following suit on lap 16.

Opposite top: 2 July 1960 – The night before the *Grand Prix de l'ACF*, Reims-Gueux – Vanwall mechanics Len Butler (crouching far left), John Wallace, Doug Orchard and Cyril Atkins tend their latest and last front-engined charge, the new 'Lowline' Vanwall 'VW11', to be driven on the morrow by Tony Brooks. He had qualified it fourteenth fastest on the starting grid, his best time 6.5 secs slower than Brabham's Cooper on pole. The transmission failed on lap eight and Vanwall's racing finally ceased the following year after one lone outing with a new rear-engined 'VW14', a 2.6-litre car known as 'The Whale,' in the Intercontinental Formula International Trophy race at Silverstone on 6 May 1961. Driven by John Surtees, it finished fifth. Here 'VW11' shows off its multi-tubular spaceframe construction with the low-level hoop behind the cockpit demonstrating the low-slung new body lines. Note the capacious midship fuel tanks secured by bungee cords, all-independent coil-spring suspension, cast alloy wheels front and rear, inboard ventilated disc brakes on the transaxle cheeks and the bright machined ball-grip of the right-hand gearchange. A great name was passing.

Overleaf: 4 September 1960 – Italian Grand Prix, Monza – Ferraris up the wall as times are clearly changing for the men from Maranello too; Willy Mairesse leading the way in Dino 246/60 chassis '0006' and Wolfgang 'Taffy' von Trips running just above the Belgian's slipstream in the rear-engined prototype Formula 2 car, chassis '0008'. This Dino 156'P' had formerly made its début in the Monaco Grand Prix on 29 May when it was equipped with a full-sized 246 V6 Formula 1 engine and was driven by test driver Richie Ginther to finish sixth. Subsequently re-engined with a 1500 cc Formula 2 unit, the rear-engined prototype was entrusted to von Trips for the Formula 2 *Solituderennen* outside Stuttgart on 24 July, which the popular German Count won, trouncing local works Porsche opposition. This Italian Grand Prix outing was '0008's' third race and von Trips finished fifth – and first in Formula 2 – while Phil Hill, Richie Ginther and Mairesse's front-engined sister cars dominated the Grand Prix, finishing 1-2-3. Unfortunately this flattering result was obtained in face of merely private-owner opposition, as Cooper, Lotus, BRM and the Walker Cooper team all boycotted the event in protest at the use of Monza's bumpy and dangerous combination banked and road circuit course.

1961

LIFE AFTER DEATH

As the dust of the 2½-litre Formula finally settled, the CSI's replacement 1½-litre Formula 1 got under way, catering for much smaller cars than hitherto with a high minimum weight limit. This new Formula had been greeted with howls of outraged dismay from British constructors when it was first announced by CSI President Auguste Pérouse at the end of the 1958 season. But while they spent much of 1959 and 1960 fighting to change the governing body's mind, Ferrari and Porsche – from Formula 2 – quietly got on with preparing new rear-engined designs with V6 water-cooled and flat-4 and flat-8 air-cooled engines respectively to race in the new Grand Prix series of 1961.

The British establishment rather foolishly proposed and backed instead an InterContinental Formula with a capacity ceiling of 3-litres. This was intended to attract American support and to prolong the life of existing 2½-litre Formula-based equipment. By the latter part of 1960, it was obvious that InterContinental racing was going to be a dead-duck. Even so, by the time the interested Formula 1 engine suppliers, Coventry Climax and BRM, finally buckled down to detailed 1½-litre engine development, they were already too late to have anything effective ready for the start of the new Formula. Coventry Climax provided stop-gap engines in the shape of a Mark II version of the FPF 1500cc Formula 1 twin-cam unit, some of which BRM bought for its own works cars pending completion of their fuel-injected V8. Climax's V8 engine appeared first, for Cooper at the 1961 German Grand Prix, the BRM V8 following in practice for the Italian event at Monza.

Only one front-engined new Formula 1 car was built, the last of the configuration's long series which had dominated Grand Prix racing from its inception. This was the four-wheel drive Ferguson-Climax Project 99, which was essentially a test and research vehicle developed to prove and promote the Ferguson four-wheel-drive system. It competed first with a 2.5-litre FPF engine in the InterContinental British Empire Trophy race at Silverstone on 8 July 1961, but then with a 1½-litre FPF installed it reappeared in the British Grand Prix at Aintree. On both occasions it was driven by Jack Fairman. Subsequently, Stirling Moss drove it in the non-Championship Oulton Park Gold Cup, which he won on a part-damp track, completely mastering the rear-engined cars. This extraordinary and singular success marked the final appearance of any front-engined Grand Prix car in a significant premier-Formula race. It was truly the end of an era which in some ways had started way back at the very birth of motoring

competition – with Emile Levassor's Paris-Bordeaux-winning Panhard of 1894. It was certainly a deliciously nose-thumbing manner in which to bow out – at the top, winning. None could ask more.

When the 1961 World Championship of Drivers ended, not a single point had been scored by anyone driving a car with an engine mounted ahead of them. The old order had finally been swept away: at top level the Dinosaurs had become extinct.

The Front-Engined Cars Competing – 1961

(INTERCONTINENTAL FORMULA): Aston Martin DBR4/250-300; Ferguson-Climax P99; Scarab
(SIGNIFICANT-LEVEL FORMULA 1): Ferguson-Climax P99.

8 July 1961 – British Empire Trophy, Silverstone – Début at this Intercontinental Formula race for the Harry Ferguson Research Ltd experimental vehicle, the Ferguson-Climax Project 99 whose coil-and-wishbone front suspension is seen here, demonstrating the outlandish manner in which the front wheel drive-shafts ran through constant-velocity joints to enter the hubs through high-level lower wishbone ends. For this Intercontinental Formula race the car was fitted with a full 2½-litre Coventry Climax FPF 4-cylinder engine, the carburettor bulge on the bonnet side needing the extension visible here to house the big 58 mm Weber carburettors. The car was entered by Rob Walker, hence the Scots midnight-blue and white livery, and was driven by trusted test driver Jack Fairman. He qualified it eleventh on the grid, 5.2 secs off John Surtees' pole-winning time in Vandervell's rear-engined Vanwall 'VW14' which finished second, but the P99 sadly retired with gearbox problems on the opening lap.

15 July 1961 – British Grand Prix, Aintree – Front-engine farewell to World Championship racing from the Fergie P99, driven here by Jack Fairman during the rain-swept opening stages, its nose having already suffered some minor damage in the hurly-burly of the opening laps. It was in conditions such as these that four-wheel-drive could really come into its own. Note the smaller carburettor cowl possible with the 1½-litre Formula 1 engine installed here, the suspension and drive-shaft layout and the new 1961 Formula regulation roll-over bar protected from possible damage by the driver's helmet, which projects above it. After his own Walker team Lotus 18/21 retired, Moss took over the P99 as the circuit began to dry and promptly lapped fast enough to frighten the opposition and get himself disqualified! Even so, he had experienced enough of the P99's unique capabilities to want to race it seriously, somewhere.

Top inset: 23 September 1961 – Gold Cup, Oulton Park – Front-engined finale in grand style as Stirling Moss's matchless skills conduct the Walker-entered Ferguson-Climax P99 to victory in its last Formula 1 appearance. On a slippery track alternately swept by light rain showers and dried by a gusting wind, Moss was able to take the lead from Graham Hill's BRM-Climax after just six laps, then simply drive away from all rear-engined opposition, eventually to beat the works Coopers of Jack Brabham and Bruce McLaren by over 40 secs. In practice he had qualified the Fergie second fastest, 0.2 sec slower than McLaren and the same margin faster than Hill, and by the end of this extraordinary race he had also set a new lap record for 1½-litre Formula 1 cars of 1:46.4, 150.7km/h (93.42mph). This was no surprise since such cars had never raced before on the Cheshire circuit, but nonetheless impressive since a representative British works-team field was present to be beaten.

Note here the four-wheel-drive sausage's low-slung form, its perforated-disc Dunlop wheels, the cranked roll-over bar, and Moss's supremely relaxed driving style even – as here – when braking very hard indeed.

Bottom inset: The cockpit of the Ferguson-Climax P99, the final front-engined Grand Prix car to be built and raced successfully, really demonstrates virtually the minimum possible size considering there is a full-length transmission shaft extending alongside the driver beneath the gearchange. The driver was slightly offset by the transmission tunnel, but why were the Maserati 250F, Vanwall, BRM 25 or even the Lotus 16 not equally compact? As 'proper' Grand Prix cars, they needed greater fuel tankage, of course, but no more room was necessary for the driver who simply rattled around within those more capacious cars. The instruments which faced Fairman and Moss present front and rear differential and centre 4WD torque-split unit temperatures (ahead of the gearchange), in addition to the normal oil and water temperatures, oil pressure and tachometer. Hereafter the forward view over a bulged bonnet to clear cylinder heads, carburettors, fuel injection trumpets and exhaust system would become a thing of antiquity. The day of the front-engined Grand Prix car had at last passed . . .

APPENDIX 1

THE FRONT-ENGINED SUCCESSES, 1945-1961
RACE WINS – POLE POSTIONS – FASTEST LAPS

This Appendix lists all significant Formula 1 races – and many not so significant – which were run, and won by front-engined GP cars, between 1945 and the last success for such a vehicle in 1961. Races which we consider to have been of truly *Grande Épreuve* status 1945-1949 and subsequent World Championship-qualifying rounds 1950-60 are introduced in capital letters. PP = Pole Position with lap time, FL = Fastest Lap with lap time, n/a = not available despite research.

(To convert miles to kilometres and mph to kph, multiply by 1.62).

1946

22 April – Nice GP, F – 65 laps, 129.81 miles
Maserati 4CL *Luigi Villoresi* 2:00:04.6 64.86 mph
PP – *Villoresi*, 1:45.0; FL – Alfa Romeo 308 *Raymond Sommer* 1:44.8, 68.60 mph

13 May – Marseilles GP, F – Two Heats, 15-lap, 33.44-miles each; Final, 35 laps, 78.03-miles
Heat One: Maserati 4CL *René Mazaud* 34:12.0, 58.66 mph
Heat Two: Maserati 4CL *Raymond Sommer* 33:26.0, 60.01 mph
Final: Maserati 4CL *Raymond Sommer* 1:20:37.7, 58.40 mph
PP – **Heat One**, Maserati 4CL *Arialdo Ruggeri*; **Heat Two**, Maserati 4CL *Tazio Nuvolari*; **Final**, *Sommer* (n/a); FL – *Nuvolari* in Heat Two, 2:06.7, 63.34 mph, *Sommer* in Final 2:09.5, 61.97 mph.

19 May – GP du Forez, St Étienne, F – 30 laps, 58.49 miles
Maserati 4CL *Raymond Sommer* 1:18:18.9, 67.94 mph
PP – n/a; FL – *Sommer*, 2:31.7, 70.80 mph

30 May – Coupe de la Résistance, Bois de Boulogne, Paris, F – 47 laps, 93.45 miles
Alfa Romeo 308 *Jean-Pierre Wimille* 1:17:41.1, 72.03 mph
PP – Maserati 4CL *Raymond Sommer*, n/a; FL – *Sommer*, 1:33.6, 75.71 mph

8 June – Coupe René Le Bègue, St Cloud, Paris, F – 30 laps, 111.84 miles
Maserati 4CL *Raymond Sommer* 1:38:42.0. 67.00 mph
PP – Sommer, 2:59.3; FL – Alfa Romeo 158 *Dr Giuseppe Farina*, 3:08.4, 71.24 mph

30 June – GP du Roussillon, Perpignan, F – 58 laps, 93.70 miles
Alfa Romeo 308 *Jean-Pierre Wimille* 1:36:31.6, 58.24 mph
PP – n/a; FL – Maserati 4CL *Raymond Sommer*, 1:38.2, 59.23 mph

7 July – GP de Bourgogne, Dijon, F – 100 laps, 128.0 miles
Alfa Romeo 308 *Jean-Pierre Wimille* 2:17:32.9, 55.83 mph
PP – n/a: FL – Wimille, 1:18.4, 58.85 mph

14 July – GP d'Albi, Les Planques, F – Aggregate of Two Heats, 16 laps each, total 176.99 miles
Heat One: Maserati 4CL *Tazio Nuvolari* 58:00.7, 91.32 mph
Heat Two: Maserati 4CL *Luigi Villoresi* 56:35.8, 93.61 mph
Aggregate Overall: Maserati 4CL *Nuvolari* – (2nd in Heat Two), 1:55:45.6, 91.57 mph
PP – n/a: FL – *Villoresi* (in Heat Two), 3:22.3, 98.20 mph

21 July – GP des Nations, Geneva, CH – Two 32-lap, 59.39-mile Heats, Final of 44 laps, 81.66 miles
Heat One: Alfa Romeo 158 *Jean-Pierre Wimille* 59:45.5, 59.15 mph
Heat Two: Alfa Romeo 158 *Dr Giuseppe Farina* 56:17.2, 62.80 mph
Final: Alfa Romeo 158 *Farina*, 1:15:49.4, 64.10 mph
PP – **Heat One**, *Wimille*; **Heat Two**, *Farina*, **Final**, *Farina* (no times found); FL – *Wimille*, 1:36.4, 68.76 mph

28 July – Prix des 24 Heures du Mans, Nantes, F – 45 laps, 115.20 miles
Maserati 4CL *'Georges Raph'* (*Raphael Bethenod de las Casas.*) 1:47:28.4, 64.07 mph
PP – n/a; FL – Alfa Romeo 308 *Jean-Pierre Wimille*, 2:13.0, 69.02 mph

25 August – Circuit des Trois Villes, Lille, F – 48 laps, 156.96 miles
Maserati 4CL *Raymond Sommer/Henri Louveau* 2:26:16.5, 64.38 mph PP – n/a; FL – *Sommer*, 2:30.9, 68.83 mph

1 September – Gran Premio del Valentino, Valentino Park, Turin, I – 60 laps, 167.76 miles
Alfa Romeo 158 *Achille Varzi* 2:35:45.8, 64.62 mph
PP – Alfa Romeo 158 *Dr Giuseppe Farina* n/a; FL – Alfa Romeo 158 *Jean-Pierre Wimille*, 1:36.8, 73.58 mph

23 September – Gran Premio di Milano, Sempione Park, Milan, I – Two 20-lap, 34.73-mile Heats, 30-lap, 52.10-mile Final
Heat One: Alfa Romeo 158 *Achille Varzi* 38.14.8, 52.38 mph
Heat Two: Alfa Romeo 158 *Consalvo Sanesi* 38:38.0, 53.92 mph
Final: Alfa Romeo 158 *Count Trossi* 56:06.0, 55.59 mph
PP – n/a for Heats, *Varzi* in Final; FL – Alfa Romeo 158s shared *Varzi* and *Farina*, 1:50, 56.70 mph

3 October – GP du Salon, Bois de Boulogne, Paris, F – 80 laps, 146.32 miles
Maserati 4CL *Raymond Sommer* 2:12:39.7, 71.67 mph
PP – n/a: FL – *Sommer*, 1:35.4, 74.88 mph

27 October – GP do Peña Rhin, Pedralbes, Barcelona, E – 80-laps, 223.18 miles
Maserati 4CL *Giorgio Pelassa* 2:46:52.0, 80.25 mph
PP – n/a; FL – n/a

1947

7 April – GP de Pau, F – 110 laps, 189.27 miles
Maserati 4CL *Nello Pagani* 3:38:31.0, 51.94 mph
PP – Maserati 4CL *Raymond Sommer*, 1:49.2: FL – Pagani, 1:51.4, 55.61 mph

27 April – GP du Roussillon, Perpignan, F – 58 laps, 91.48 miles
Talbot-Lago Monoplace 1938 *Eugène Chaboud* 1:35:06.3, 57.67 mph
PP – n/a; FL – Maserati 4CL *Raymond Sommer*, 1:34.2, 60.24 mph

8 May – Jersey Road Race, St Helier, CI – 50 laps, 160.00 miles
Maserati 4CL *Reg Parnell* 1:53:33.0, 84.52 mph
PP – Maserati 4CL 'B.Bira' *(Prince Birabongse Bhanubandh)*, 2:06.4; FL – Maserati 4CL *Raymond Sommer*, 2:06.2, 91.28 mph

18 May – Marseille GP, F – 69 laps, 188.65 miles
Talbot-Lago *Eugène Chaboud* 2:50:23.6, 66.42 mph
PP – n/a; FL – Maserati 4CL *Luigi Villoresi*, 2:17.2, 71.74 mph

1 June – Nîmes GP, F – 70 laps, 228.86 miles
Maserati 4CL *Luigi Villoresi* 3:39:59.4, 62.10 mph
PP – n/a; FL – *Villoresi*, 3:00.9, 63.86 mph

8 June – SWISS GRAND PRIX, Bremgarten, Bern, CH – Two 20-lap, 90.27-mile Heats, 30-lap, 135.60-mile Final
Heat One: Alfa Romeo 158 *Achille Varzi* 1:03:37.5, 85.80 mph
Heat Two: Alfa Romeo 158 *Jean-Pierre Wimille* 57:46.3, 94.50 mph
Final: Alfa Romeo 158 *Jean-Pierre Wimille* 1:25:09.1, 96.18 mph
PP – Heat One, Alfa Romeo 158 *Count Carlo Trossi*, 2:42.9; Heat Two, Alfa Romeo 158 *Wimille* time n/a; Final, 2*Wimille*; FL – Heat One, *Varzi*, 3:02.3, 89.13 mph; Heat Two, Maserati 4CL *Raymond Sommer*, 2:46.6, 98.30 mph; Final, *Wimille*, 2:47.0, 98.06 mph

29 June – BELGIAN GRAND PRIX, Spa-Francorchamps, B – 35 laps, 305.98 miles
Alfa Romeo 158 *Jean-Pierre Wimille* 3:18:28.64, 95.28 mph
PP – *Wimille*, no time found; FL – *Wimille*, 5:18.0, 101.94 mph

6 July – GP de la Marne, Reims-Gueux, F – 51 laps, 246.36 miles
Maserati 4CL *Christian Kautz* 2:34:50.7, 95.80 mph
PP – n/a; FL – Maserati 4CL, 2:52.2, 100.99 mph

13 July – GP d'Albi, Les Planques, F – 40 laps, 220.80 miles
Talbot-Lago Type 26C *Louis Rosier* 2:29:48.7, 88.41 mph
PP – Maserati 4CL *Henri Louveau*, time n/a; FL – Maserati 4CL *Luigi Villoresi*, 3:26.4, 96.25 mph

13 July – Bari GP, I – 50 laps, 165.91 miles
Alfa Romeo 158 *Achille Varzi* 2:32:13.8, 65.39 mph
PP – n/a; FL – *Varzi*, 2:49.0, 70.68 mph

20 July – Nice GP, F – 100 laps, 199.71 miles
Maserati 4CL *Luigi Villoresi* 3:07:07.1, 63.92 mph
PP – *Villoresi*, 1:43.3; FL – Maserati 4CL *Raymond Sommer*, 1:44.0, 69.08 mph

3 August – GP d'Alsace, Strasbourg, F – 85 laps, 191.58 miles
Maserati 4CL *Luigi Villoresi* 2:45:41.9, 69.37 mph
PP – *Villoresi*, 1:49.5; FL – *Villoresi*, 1:47.2, 75.95 mph

9 August – Ulster Trophy, Ballyclare, NI – 36 laps, 149.11 miles
ERA B-Type *Bob Gerard* 2:05:10.0, 71.48 mph
PP – *Gerard* 3:11.0; FL – *Gerard*, 3:14.0, 76.76 mph

10 August – GP du Comminges, F – 30 laps, 205.05 miles
Talbot-Lago Monoplace 1938 *Louis Chiron* 2:35:37.4, 78.74 mph
PP – n/a; FL – Maserati 4CL *Dorino Serafini*, 4:15.5, 96.31 mph

21 August – British Empire Trophy, Douglas, Isle of Man, GB – 40 laps, 155.12 miles
ERA B-Type *Bob Gerard* 2:16:52, 68.02 mph
PP – Maserati 4CL 'B. Bira', 3:16, FL – *Gerard*, 3:18, 70.53 mph

7 September – ITALIAN GRAND PRIX, Sempione Park, Milan – 100 laps, 214.25 miles
Alfa Romeo 158 *Count Carlo Trossi* 3:02:25.0, 70.29 mph
PP – Alfa Romeo 158 *Consalvo Sanesi*, 1:44.0; FL – Trossi, 3:02:25.0

21 September – GRAND PRIX DE L'ACF, Lyons-Parilly, F – 70 laps, 317.13 miles
Talbot Monoplace 1938 *Louis Chiron* 4:03:40.7, 78.09 mph
PP – Maserati 4CL *Henri Louveau*; FL – Maserati 4CLs 'Georges Raph' and *Luigi Villoresi*, 3:17.5, 82.40 mph

5 October – GP de Lausanne, CH – 90 laps, 181.86 miles
Maserati 4CL *Luigi Villoresi* 2:49:30.4, 93.92 mph
PP – n/a; FL – Maserati 4CL *Alberto Ascari*, 1:46.5, 68.35 mph

4 November – Coupe du Salon, Montlhéry, Paris, F – 48 laps, 187.41 miles
Talbot offset monoplace 1939 *Yves Giraud-Cabantous* 2:06:28.2, 88.75 mph
PP – n/a; FL – Maserati 4CL *Raymond Sommer*, 2:29.4, 90.92 mph

1948

29 March – GP de Pau, F – 110 laps, 193.71 miles
Maserati 4CL *Nello Pagani* 3:33:30.0, 54.43 mph
PP – Simca-Gordini *Jean-Pierre Wimille*, 1:49.7; FL – *Wimille*, 1:52.6, 56.29 mph

29 April – Jersey Road Race, St Helier, CI – 55 laps, 176.00 miles
ERA B-Type *Bob Gerard* 2:00:55.2, 87.83 mph
PP – Maserati 4CL *'B. Bira'*, 2:01.4; FL – *Gerard*, 2:07.4, 90.42 mph

2 May – GP des Nations, Geneva, CH – 80 laps, 146.40 mph
Maserati 4CL *Dr Giuseppe Farina* 2:23:58.2, 61.38 mph
PP – n/a; FL – *Farina*, 1:44.1, 63.86 mph

16 May – MONACO GRAND PRIX, Monte Carlo – 100 laps, 195.40 miles
Maserati 4CL *Dr Giuseppe Farina* 3:18:26.9, 59.74 mph
PP – Farina, 1:53.8; FL – *Farina*, 1:53.9, 62.67 mph

25 May – British Empire Trophy, Douglas, Isle of Man, GB – 36 laps, 139.68 miles
ERA B-Type *Geoffrey Ansell* 2:03:45, 67.69 mph
PP – ERA B-Type *Bob Gerard*, 3:10; FL – shared Maserati 4CL *Reg Parnell* and ERA E-Type *Leslie Johnson*, 3:13, 72.35 mph

30 May – GP de Paris, Montlhéry, F – 50 laps, 195.73 miles
Talbot offset monoplace 1939 *Yves Giraud-Cabantous* 2:08:52.2, 82.30 mph
PP – n/a; FL – *Giraud-Cabantous*, 2:29.8, 94.10 mph

27 June – GP di San Remo, 85 laps, 176.19 miles
Maserati 4CLT/48 *Alberto Ascari* 3:03:34.0, 58.95 mph
PP – Maserati 4CL *Dr Giuseppe Farina*, time n/a; FL – Maserati 4CLT/48 *Luigi Villoresi*, 2:02.6, 61.75 mph

4 July – SWISS GRAND PRIX, Bremgarten, Basle, CH – 40 laps, 180.50 miles
Alfa Romeo 158 *Count Carlo Trossi* 1:59:17.3, 90.81 mph
PP – Alfa Romeo 158 *Jean-Pierre Wimille*, 2:42.5; FL – *Wimille*, 2:51.0, 95.05 mph

18 July – GRAND PRIX DE L'ACF, Reims-Gueux – 64 laps, 109.16 miles
Alfa Romeo 158 *Jean-Pierre Wimille* 3:01:07.5, 102.96 mph
PP – *Wimille*, 2:35.2; FL – *Wimille*, 2:41.2, 108.13 mph

7 August – Grote Prijs van Nederland, Zandvoort – Two 24-lap, 63.40-mile Heats; 40-lap, 104.0-mile Final
Heat One: Maserati 4CL *Reg Parnell*, 50.17.8, 75.63 mph
Heat Two: Maserati 4CL *'B. Bira'*, 50:24.3, 75.47 mph
Final: Maserati 4CL *'B. Bira'*, 1:25:22.2, 73.09 mph
PP – Heat One, ERA B/C-Type *Cuthbert Harrison*, 2:03.8; Heat Two – Maserati 4CL *'B. Bira'*, 2:00.2; Final, by ballot, Maserati 4C *Anthony Baring*; FL – Heat One, ERA B-Type *John Bolster*, 1:57.9, 79.39 mph' Heat Two ' *'B. Bira'*, 1:53.6, 79.59 mph; Final – n/a

8 August – GP de Comminges, F – 30 laps, 205.15 mph
Maserati 4CLT/48 *Luigi Villoresi* 2:11:45.5, 93.40 mph
PP – *Villoresi*, 4:02.3; FL – *Villoresi*, 4:12.8, 97.38 mph

29 August – GP d'Albi, Les Planques, F – Aggregate of two 17-lap Heats, 187.62 miles
Heat One: Maserati 4CLT/48 *Luigi Villoresi* 56:19.9, 100.17 mph
Heat Two: Maserati 4CLT/48 *Luigi Villoresi* 56:38.0, 99.38 mph
PP – Heat One, *Villoresi*, 3:14.2, Heat Two: *Villoresi*; FL – Heat One, *Villoresi*, 3:10.7, 104.42 mph; Heat Two, n/a

5 September – ITALIAN GRAND PRIX, Monza – 75 laps, 223.75 miles
Alfa Romeo 158 *Jean-Pierre Wimille* 3:10:42.4, 70.38 mph
PP – *Wimille*, time n/a; FL – *Wimille*, 2:22.4, 75.41 mph

2 October – BRITISH GRAND PRIX, Silverstone – 65 laps, 238.89 miles
Maserati 4CLT/48 *Luigi Villoresi* 3:18:03, 72.28 mph
PP – Talbot-Lago Type 26C *Louis Chiron*, 2:56.0*; FL – *Villoresi*, 2:52.0, 77.73 mph
(*In the absence of the *Villoresi* and *Ascari* Scuderia Ambrosiana Maserati 4CLT/48s which arrived late)

10 October – GP du Salon, Montlhéry, Paris, F – 48 laps, 186.41 miles
Talbot-Lago Type 26C *Louis Rosier* 2:03:52.9, 90.56 mph
PP – n/a; FL – Maserati 4CL *'B. Bira'*, 2:25.9, 96.34 mph

17 October – GP dell'Autodromo di Monza, Milan, I – 80 laps, 313.17 miles
Alfa Romeo 158 *Jean-Pierre Wimille* 2:50:44.4, 110.05 mph
PP – *Wimille*, 1:59.3; FL – Alfa Romeo 158 *Consalvo Sanesi* 2:00.4, 117.05 mph

24 October – Circuito di Garda, Lago di Garda, I – 18 laps, 183.13 miles
Ferrari 125 *Dr Giuseppe Farina* 2:30:49.8, 72.85 mph
PP – n/a; FL – n/a

31 October – Grand Premio do Peña Rhin, Pedralbes, Barcelona, E – 70 laps, 194.08 miles
Maserati 4CLT/48, *Luigi Villoresi*, 2:10:12, 89.44 mph
PP – n/a; FL – *Villoresi*, 1:46, 94.16 mph

1949

**3 April – Gran Premio di San Remo, Ospedaletti, I –
Aggregate of two 45-lap Heats, 186.55 miles**
Heat One: Maserati 4CLT/48 *Juan Fangio* 1:31:33.4, 61.16
mph
Heat Two: Maserati 4CLT/48 *Juan Fangio* 1:29:55.2 62.20
mph
Aggregate: *Fangio*, 3:01:28.6, 61.68 mph

**18 April – Richmond Trophy, Goodwood, GB – 10 laps,
23.80 miles**
Maserati 4CLT/48 *Reg Parnell*, 17:22.4, 82.89 mph
PP – by ballot, Maserati 4CL *Reg Ansell*; FL – *Parnell*,
1:40.2, 86.23 mph

18 April – GP de Pau, F – 110 laps, 193.71 miles
Maserati 4CLT/48 *Juan Fangio*, 3:36:11.9, 53.76 mph
PP – *Fangio*, 1:47.3; FL – *Fangio*, 1:49.0, 56.65 mph

24 April – GP de Paris, Montlhéry, F – 50 laps, 195.73 miles
Talbot-Lago Type 26C *Philippe Étancelin* 2:05:31.8, 93.12
mph
PP – n/a; FL – Simca-Gordini *Louis Rosier*, 2:24.8, 97.32
mph

**28 April – Jersey Road Race, St Helier, CI – 55 laps, 176.00
miles**
ERA B-Type *Bob Gerard* 2:16:58.6, 77.10 mph
PP – Maserati 4CLT/48 *Luigi Villoresi*, 2:00.0; FL – *Villoresi*, 2:08.1, 89.93 mph

**7 April – GP du Roussillon, Perpignan, F – Aggregate of
two 50-lap Heats, 157.60 miles**
Heat One: Maserati 4CLS/48 *Juan Fangio* 1:17:06.8, 61.36
mph
Heat Two: Maserati 4CLT/48 *'B. Bira'* 1:16:09.4, 62.13 mph
Aggregate: *Fangio*, 2:33:16.7, 61.74 mph
PP – Heat One, n/a; Heat Two, n/a; FL – Heat One,
Fangio, 1:29.2, 63.61 mph; Heat Two, n/a

**14 April – BRITISH GRAND PRIX, Silverstone – 100
laps, 300 miles**
Maserati 4CLT/48 *Baron Emmanuel de Graffenried*,
2:52:50.2, 77.31 mph
PP – Maserati 4CLT/48 *Luigi Villoresi*, 2:09.8; FL – Maserati 4CLT/48 *'B. Bira'*, 2:10.4, 82.82 mph

**26 April – British Empire Trophy, Douglas, Isle of Man,
GB – 36 laps, 139.68 miles**
ERA B-Type *Bob Gerard* 1:57:56, 71.06 mph
PP – Maserati 4CLT/48 *Reg Parnell*, 3:06; FL – n/a

**5 June – GP des Frontières, Chimay, B – 15 laps, 101.31
miles**
Talbot-Lago Type 26C *Guy Mairesse* 1:10:20.0, 86.43 mph
PP – *Mairesse*, time n/a; FL – *Mairesse*, 4:32.6, 89.21 mph

**19 June – BELGIAN GRAND PRIX, Spa-Francorchamps
– 35 laps, 314.87 miles**
Talbot-Lago Type 26C *Louis Rosier* 3:15:17, 96.95 mph
PP – n/a; FL – Maserati 4CLT/48 *Dr Giuseppe Farina*, 5:19,
101.64 mph

**3 July – SWISS GRAND PRIX*, Bremgarten, Berne – 40
laps, 180.50 miles**
Ferrari 125 *Alberto Ascari*, 1:59:24.6
PP – Maserati 4CLT/48 *Dr Giuseppe Farina*, 2:50.4; FL
– Farina, 2:52.2, 94.34 mph
(*Despite its surprisingly short distance, any Swiss GP on
the daunting Bremgarten forest circuit well merited *Grande
Épreuve* status)

**10 July – GP d'Albi, Les Planques, F – One 5-lap,
27.59-mile Heat, 34-lap final, 187.62 miles**
Heat: Maserati 4CLT/48 *Juan Fangio* 16:20.4, 101.37 mph
Final: Maserati 4CLT/48 *Juan Fangio* 1:54:38.6, 98.19 mph
PP – Heat, *Fangio*, 3:11.9; Final (decided by finish order
in Heat), *Fangio*; FL – Heat n/a, Final, 3:14.4, 102.17 mph

**17 July – GRAND PRIX DE FRANCE, Reims-Gueux –
64 laps, 309.16 miles**
Talbot-Lago Type 26C *Louis Chiron* 3:02:33.7, 99.96 mph
PP – Gerrari 125 *Luigi Villoresi* time n/a; FL – Ferrari
125 *Peter Whitehead*, 2:46.2, 105.20 mph

**31 July – Grote Prijs van Zandvoort, NL – Two 25-lap,
65-mile Heats, 40-lap Final, 104.00 miles**
Heat One: Ferrari 125 *Luigi Villoresi* 51:29.2, 75.92 mph
Heat Two: Maserati 4CLT/48 *Reg Parnell* 52:30.2, 74.44
mph
Final: Ferrari 125 *Luigi Villoresi* 1:21:06.9, 77.12 mph
PP – Heat One, Maserati 4CLT/48 *Dr Giuseppe Farina*,
1:54.8; Heat Two, Ferrari 125 *Alberto Ascari*, 1:55.0; Final
(decided on Heat winning times), *Villoresi*; FL – Heat One,
Villoresi, 1:59.3, 78.46 mph; Heat Two, *Ascari*, 2:01.7, 77.07
mph; Final, *Parnell*, 1:57.8, 79.62 mph

**20 August – BRDC International Trophy, Silverstone, GB
– Two 20-lap, 60-mile Heats, 30-lap Final, 90.00 miles**
Heat One: Maserati 4CLT/48 *'B. Bira'* 39:00.2, 91.43 mph
Heat Two: Maserati 4CLT/48 *Dr Giuseppe Farina* 39:44.4,
89.73 mph
Final: Ferrari 125 *Alberto Ascari* 59:42.6, 90.44 mph
PP – Heat One, Ascari, 1:56.0; Heat Two, Maserati
4CLT/48 *Baron Emmanuel de Graffenried*, 1:55.0; Final, FL
– n/a

27 August – GP de Lausanne, CH – 90 laps, 181.86 miles
Maserati 4CLT/48 *Dr Giuseppe Farina* 2:44:27.3, 65.81 mph
PP – n/a; FL – n/a

**11 September – ITALIAN GRAND PRIX, Monza – 80
laps, 313.17 miles**
Ferrari 125 *Alberto Ascari* 2:58:53.6, 105.04 mph
PP – *Ascari*, 2:05.0; FL – *Ascari*, 2:06.8, 111.35 mph

17 September – Goodwood Trophy, GB – 10 laps, 23.80 miles
Maserati 4CLT/48 *Reg Parnell* 16:39.6, 86.43 mph
PP – (by ballot) Cooper-JAP 1100* *Stirling Moss*; FL – Parnell, 1:36.8, 89.26 mph
(*Note this first appearance of a rear-engined car in our listing, achieved at the time purely by the luck of the draw, rather than by performance . . .)

25 September – Masaryk Grand Prix, Brno, Cz – 20 laps, 221.22 miles
Ferrari 125 *Peter Whitehead* 2:48:41.0, 78.72 mph
PP – n/a; FL – shared Maserati 4CLT/48s *Baron Emmanuel de Graffenried* and *'B. Bira'*, 8:03.0, 82.29 mph

9 October – GP du Salon, Montlhéry, Paris, F – 64 laps, 249.88 miles
Talbot-Lago Type 26C *Raymond Sommer* 2:42:18, 92.38 mph
PP – n/a; FL – *Sommer*, 2:23.8, 97.53 mph

1950

10 April – Grand Prix de Pau, F – 110 laps, 193.71 miles
Maserati 4CLT/50 *Juan Fangio* 3:14:20.0, 58.06 mph
PP – *Fangio*, 1:43.1; FL – *Fangio*, 1:42.8, 61.67 mph

10 April – Richmond Trophy, Goodwood, GB – 11 laps, 26.40 miles
Maserati 4CLT/48 *Reg Parnell* 20:14.4, 78.26 mph

16 April – Gran Premio di San Remo, Ospedaletti, I – 90 laps, 186.55 miles
Alfa Romeo 158 *Juan Fangio* 3:10:08, 59.59 mph
PP – n/a; FL – Ferrari 125 *Luigi Villoresi* 2:00.0, 62.33 mph

30 April – Grand Prix de Paris, Montlhéry, F – 50 laps, 195.73 miles
Talbot-Lago Type 26C *Georges Grignard* 2:05:38.8, 93.37 mph
PP – n/a; FL – Talbot-Lago Type 26C *Raymond Sommer*, 2:20.5, 100.19 mph

13 May – BRITISH GRAND PRIX, Silverstone – 70 laps, 210.00 miles
Alfa Romeo 158 *Dr Giuseppe Farina* 2:13:23.6, 90.95 mph
PP – Farina, 1:50.8; FL – *Farina*, 1:50.6, 94.02 mph

21 May – MONACO GRAND PRIX, Monte Carlo – 100 laps, 195.41 miles
Alfa Romeo 158 *Juan Fangio* 3:13:18.7, 61.33 mph
PP – *Fangio*, 1:50.2; FL – *Fangio*, 1:51.0, 64.09 mph

15 June – British Empire Trophy, Douglas, Isle of Man, GB – 36 laps, 139.68 miles
ERA B-Type *Bob Gerard* 1:59:36.8, 70.07 mph
PP – *Gerard*, time n/a; FL – Maserati 4CLT/48 *Reg Parnell*, 3:08.0, 74.30 mph

4 June – SWISS GRAND PRIX, Bremgarten, Bern – 42 laps, 189.53 miles
Alfa Romeo 158 *Dr Giuseppe Farina* 2:02:53.7, 92.76 mph
PP – Alfa Romeo 158 *Juan Fangio*, 2:42.1; FL – *Farina*, 2:41.6, 100.78 mph

18 June – BELGIAN GRAND PRIX, Spa-Francorchamps – 35 laps, 307.10 miles
Alfa Romeo 158 *Juan Fangio* 2:47:26.0, 110.05 mph
PP – Alfa Romeo 158 *Dr Giuseppe Farina*, 4:37.0; FL – *Farina*, 4:34.1, 115.40 mph

2 July – GRAND PRIX DE L'ACF, Reims-Gueux – 64 laps, 309.16 miles
Alfa Romeo 158 *Juan Fangio* 2:57:52.8, 104.28 mph
PP – *Fangio*, 2:30.6; FL – *Fangio*, 2:35.6, 112.36 mph

9 July – Gran Premio Bari, I – 35 laps, 198.83 miles
Alfa Romeo 158 *Dr Giuseppe Farina* 2:34:29.6, 77.22 mph
PP – n/a; FL – n/a

13 July – Jersey Road Race, St Helier, CI – 55 laps, 176.00 miles
Ferrari 125 *Peter Whitehead* 1:56:02.6, 90.94 mph
PP – Maserati 4CLT/48 *David Hampshire*, 2:02.4; FL – *Hampshire*, 2:02.0, 94.43 mph

17 July – GP d'Albi, Les Planques, F – Aggregate of two 17-lap, 187.62-mile heats
Heat One: Talbot-Lago Type 26C *Raymond Sommer* 55:53.6, 100.93 mph
Heat Two: Maserati 4CT/48 *Froilan Gonzalez* 56:27.7, 99.92 mph
Aggregate: Talbot-Lago 26C *Louis Rosier* 1:53:08.6, 99.67 mph
PP – n/a; FL (Heat One), Maserati 4CLT/48 *Juan Fangio*, 3:06.7, 106.65 mph

23 July – Grote Prijs van Nederland, Zandvoort, NL – 90 laps, 234.45 miles
Talbot-Lago Type 26C *Louis Rosier* 3:03:36.3, 76.62 mph
PP – Talbot-Lago Type 26C *Raymond Sommer*, 1:51.8; FL – *Sommer*, 1:52.1, 83.67 mph

30 July – GP des Nations, Geneva, CH – 68 laps, 169.05 miles
Alfa Romeo 158 *Juan Fangio* 2:07:55.0, 79.28 mph
PP – *Fangio*, time n/a; FL – Alfa Romeo 158 *Piero Taruffi*, 1:45.1, 85.14 mph

12 August – Ulster Trophy, Dundrod, NI – 15 laps, 111.24 miles
Ferrari 125 *Peter Whitehead* 1:19:09, 84.32 mph
PP – n/a; FL – *Whitehead*, 5:06.6, 87.08 mph

15 August – Gran Premio di Pescara, I – 16 laps, 256.50 miles
Alfa Romeo 158 *Juan Fangio* 3:02:51.4, 84.65 mph
PP – *Fangio*, 10:37.6; FL – *Fangio*, 10:37.6, 90.52 mph

26 August – BRDC International Trophy, Silverstone, GB – Two 15-lap, 43.36-mile Heats, 35-lap Final, 101.12 miles
Heat One: Alfa Romeo 158 *Dr Giuseppe Farina* 28:53, 93.48 mph
Heat Two: Alfa Romeo 158 *Juan Fangio* 33.53, 79.69 mph
Final: Alfa Romeo 158 *Dr Giuseppe Farina*, 1:07:17.0, 96.63 mph
PP – n/a; FL (Final), *Farina* and *Fangio*, 1:52.0, 96.43 mph

3 September – GRAN PREMIO D'ITALIA, Monza – 80 laps, 313.17 miles
Alfa Romeo 158 *Dr Giuseppe Farina* 2:51:17.4, 109.63 mph
PP – Alfa Romeo 158 *Juan Fangio*, 1:58.3; FL – *Fangio*, 2:00.0, 117.44 mph

30 September – Goodwood Trophy, GB – 12 laps, 28.56 miles
BRM Type 15 *Reg Parnell* 20:58.4, 82.48 mph
PP – (by ballot), Talbot-Lago Type 26C *Johnny Claes*; FL – *Parnell*, 1:41.8, 84.95 mph

29 October – Gran Premio do Peña Rhin, Pedralbes, Barcelona, E – 70 laps, 194.18 miles
Ferrari 375 *Alberto Ascari* 2:05:14.8, 93.02 mph
PP – n/a; FL – n/a

1951

11 March – Gran Premio di Siracusa, Sicily, I – 80 laps, 268.43 miles
Ferrari 375 *Luigi Villoresi* 2:57:31.6, 90.72 mph
PP – Ferrari 375 *Alberto Ascari* time n/a; FL – *Ascari*, 2:06.1, 95.72 mph

26 March – Richmond Trophy, Goodwood, GB – 12 laps, 28.56 miles
Maserati 4CLT/48 *'B. Bira'* 19:44.0, 87.57 mph
PP – (by ballot) ERA B-Type *Graham Whitehead*; FL – *'B. Bira'*, 1:35.6, 90.38 mph

26 March – Grand Prix de Pau, F – 110 laps, 193.60 miles
Ferrari 375 *Luigi Villoresi* 3:17:39.9, 57.45 mph
PP – Ferrari 275 *Alberto Ascari*, 1:40.8; FL – *Ascari*, 1:41.7, 60.91 mph

22 April – Gran Premio di San Remo, Ospedaletti, I – 90 laps, 186.55 miles
Ferrari 375 *Alberto Ascari* 2:57:08.2, 63.19 mph
PP – *Ascari*, 1:52.0; FL – *Ascari*, 1:53.8, 65.57 mph

29 April – Grand Prix de Bordeaux, F – 123 laps, 187.85 miles
Talbot-Lago Type 26C *Louis Rosier* 3:07:11.3, 60.21 mph
PP – n/a; FL – *Rosier*, 1:28.1, 62.41 mph

5 May – BRDC International Trophy, Silverstone, GB – Two 15-lap, 43.32-mile Heats, 35-lap Final, 101.08 miles
Heat One: Alfa Romeo 159 *Juan Fangio* 28:27, 91.38 mph
Heat Two: Alfa Romeo 159 *Dr Giuseppe Farina* 27:51, 93.35 mph
Final: Ferrari 375* *Reg Parnell* 16:48.0, 61.89 mph
(*G A Vandervell's privately-entered *Thin Wall Special* Ferrari won Final – flagged-off after only 6 laps due to torrential rain)
PP – Heat One, Alfa Romeo 159 *Felice Bonetto*, 1:58; Heat Two, Alfa Romeo 158 *Consalvo Sanesi*, 1:52; Final, *Sanesi*, FL – Heat One, *Fangio*, 1:48, 96.29 mph; Heat Two, *Farina*, 1:47, 97.19 mph; Final, *Parnell*, 2:38, 65.82 mph

20 May – Grand Prix de Paris, Montlhéry, Paris, F – 125 laps, 194.37 miles
Maserati 4CLT/48 *Dr Giuseppe Farina* 2:53:12.5, 67.33 mph
PP – n/a; FL – Simca-Gordini *Juan Fangio*, 1:18.7, 71.44 mph

27 May – SWISS GRAND PRIX, Bremgarten, Berne – 42 laps, 189.53 miles
Alfa Romeo 159 *Juan Fangio* 2:07:53.64, 89.18 mph
PP – *Fangio*, 2:35.9; FL – Fangio, 2:51.1, 95.18 mph

2 June – Ulster Trophy, Dundrod, NI – 27 laps, 200.23 miles
Alfa Romeo 159 *Dr Giuseppe Farina* 2:11:21.8, 91.46 mph
PP – Farina (time n/a); FL – *Farina*, 4:44.0, 94.01 mph

17 June – BELGIAN GRAND PRIX, Spa-Francorchamps – 36 laps, 314.72 miles
Alfa Romeo 159 *Dr Giuseppe Farina* 2:45:46.2, 114.32 mph
PP – Alfa Romeo 159 *Juan Fangio*, 4:25; FL – *Fangio*, 4:22.1, 120.51 mph

1 July – GRAND PRIX DE L'ACF, Reims-Gueux – 77 laps, 374.22 miles
Alfa Romeo 159 *Juan Fangio/Luigi Fagioli* 3:22:11.0, 110.97 mph
PP – *Fangio*, 2:25.7; FL – *Fangio*, 2:27.8, 118.29 mph

14 July – BRITISH GRAND PRIX, Silverstone – 90 laps, 259.92 miles
Ferrari 375 *Froilan Gonzalez* 2:42:18.2, 96.11 mph
PP – Gonzales, 1:43.4; FL – Alfa Romeo 159 *Dr Guiseppe Farina*, 1:44.0, 99.99 mph

21 July – 'Scottish Grand Prix', Winfield Aerodrome, GB – 50 laps, 100 miles
Maserati 4CLT/48 *Philip Fotheringham-Parker* 1:19:27.0, 75.52 mph
PP – HWM-Alta *Reg Parnell*, time n/a; FL – Alta *Joe Kelly*, 1:29.2, 80.75 mph

22 July – Grote Prijs van Nederland, Zandvoort, NL – 90 laps, 234.45 miles
Talbot-Lago Type 26C *Louis Rosier* 2:59:19.4, 78.45 mph
PP – Maserati 4CLT/48 *Dr Giuseppe Farina*, 1:52.9; FL – Talbot-Lago Type 26C *André Pilette*, 1:54.0, 82.28 mph

29 July – GERMAN GRAND PRIX, Nürburgring – 20 laps, 283.20 miles
Ferrari 375 *Alberto Ascari* 3:23:03.3, 83.80 mph
PP – Ascari, 9:55.8; FL – Alfa Romeo 159 *Juan Fangio*, 9:55.8, 85.70 mph

5 August – Grand Prix d'Albi, Les Planques, F – 34 laps, 189.15 miles
Simca-Gordini *Maurice Trintignant* 1:51:23.1, 101.87 mph
PP – n/a; FL – *Trintignant,* 3:11.6, 104.53 mph

15 August – Gran Premio di Pescara, I – 12 laps, 192.00 miles
Ferrari 375 *Froilan Gonzalez* 2:14:59.8, 85.50 mph
PP – Ferrari 375 *Alberto Ascari*, 10:43.6; FL – *Gonzalez*, 10:48.8, 88.95 mph

2 September – Gran Premio Bari, I – 65 laps, 223.67 miles
Alfa Romeo 159 *Juan Fangio* 2:39:58.3, 83.89 mph
PP – *Fangio*, 2:20.2; FL – *Fangio*, 2:20.6, 88.14 mph

16 September – GRAN PREMIO D'ITALIA, Monza – 80 laps, 312.76 miles
Ferrari 375 *Alberto Ascari* 2:42:39.3, 115.52 mph
PP – Alfa Romeo 159B *Juan Fangio*, 1:53.2; FL – Alfa Romeo 159B *Dr Giuseppe Farina*, 1:56.5, 121.49 mph

29 September – Goodwood Trophy, GB – 15 laps, 35.70 miles
Alfa Romeo 158 *Dr Giuseppe Farina* 22:31.2, 95.11 mph
PP – n/a; FL – *Farina*, 1:28.0, 97.36 mph

28 October – SPANISH GRAND PRIX, Pedralbes, Barcelona – 70 laps, 274.88 miles
Alfa Romeo 159B *Juan Fangio* 2:46:54.10, 98.82 mph
PP – Ferrari 375 *Alberto Ascari*, 2:10.59; FL – Fangio, 2:16.93, 103.24 mph

1952

6 April – Grand Premio del Valentino, Valentino Park, Turin, I – 60 laps, 156.44 miles
Ferrari 375 *Luigi Villoresi* 2:06:25.3, 74.25 mph
PP – Ferrari 375 *Dr Giuseppe Farina*, time n/a; FL – *Farina*, 2:01.1, 77.54 mph

14 April – Richmond Trophy, Goodwood, GB – 12 laps, 28.80 miles
Ferrari 375* *Froilan Gonzalez* 19:35.0, 88.23 mph
PP – *Gonzalez* (time n/a); FL – *Gonzalez*, 1:36, 90.00 mph
(*Vandervell's *Thin Wall Special*)

1 June – Grand Prix d'Albi, Les Planques, NI – 34 laps, 189.15 miles
Ferrari 375 *Louis Rosier* 1:50:39.0, 101.90 mph
PP – BRM Type 15 *Juan Fangio*, 2:54.6; FL – BRM Type 15 (*Froilan Gonzalez*), 3:06.0, 106.98 mph

7 June – Ulster Trophy, Dundrod, NI – 34 laps, 252.11 miles
Ferrari 375* *Piero Taruffi* 3:05:47.0, 81.43 mph
PP – *Taruffi*, 5:06

SEE APPENDIX 2, p.154, FOR 1952/53 F2 EVENTS

1953

31 May – Grand Prix d'Albi, Les Planques, F – Two 10-lap, 55.63-mile Heats, 18-lap Final, 100.14 miles
Heat One: BRM Type 15 *Juan Fangio* 29:57.8, 110.69 mph
Heat Two: Ferrari 375 *Louis Rosier* 33:41.4, 98.29 mph
Final: Ferrari 375 *Louis Rosier* 56:36.8, 105.45 mph
PP – Heat One, BRM Type 15 *Froilan Gonzalez* time n/a; Heat Two, *Rosier* (time n/a); Final, *Fangio*; FL – Heat One, *Fangio*, 2:52.2, 115.57 mph; Heat Two, Gordini Type 16 *Roberto Mieres*, 3:14.3, 102.41 mph; Final, *Fangio*, 2:52.3, 115.48 mph

28 June – Grand Prix de Rouen-les-Essarts, F – 60 laps, 190.14 miles
Ferrari 500 *Dr Giuseppe Farina* 2:15:05.8, 84.45 mph
PP – Farina, 2:12.2; FL – Ferrari 500 *Mike Hawthorn*, 2:12.8, 85.91 mph

1954

17 January ARGENTINE GRAND PRIX, Buenos Aires – 87 laps, 192.71 miles
Maserati *Juan Fangio* 3:00:55.8, 70.16 mph
PP – Ferrari 625 *Dr Giuseppe Farina*, 1:44.8; FL – Ferrari 625 *Froilan Gonzalez*, 1:48.2, 80.70 mph

11 April – Gran Premio Siracusa, Sicily, I – 80 laps, 278.24 miles
Ferrari 625 *Dr Giuseppe Farina* 2:51:57.2, 95.32 mph
PP – Maserati 250F *Onofre Marimon*, 2:02.6; FL – *Marimon*, 2:03.8, 99.36 mph

19 April – Grand Prix de Pau, F – 110 laps, 188.54 miles
Gordini Type 16 *Jean Behra* 3:00:02.2, 62.62 mph
PP – Ferrari 625 *Dr Giuseppe Farina*, 1:36.3; FL – *Behra*, 1:35.2, 65.06 mph

19 April – Lavant Cup, Goodwood, GB – 7 laps, 16.80 miles
Ferrari 625 *Reg Parnell* 11:21.4, 88.77 mph
PP – Maserati 250F *Roy Salvadori* time n/a; FL – *Parnell* and *Salvadori*, 1:36.2, 89.81 mph

9 May – Grand Prix de Bordeaux, F – 123 laps, 187.85 miles
Ferrari 625 *Froilan Gonzalez* 3:05:55.1, 60.62 mph
PP – Ferrari 625 *Maurice Trintignant*, 1:21.8; FL – *Gonzalez*, 1:22.7, 66.84 mph

**15 May – BRDC International Trophy, Silverstone, GB –
Two 15-lap, 43.91-mile Heats, 35-lap Final, 102.44 miles**
Heat One: Ferrari 553 *Froilan Gonzalez* 31.49, 82.79 mph
Heat Two: Ferrari 625 *Maurice Trintignant* 30:09, 87.37
mph
Final: Ferrari 625 *Froilan Gonzalez* 1:06:15, 92.78 mph
PP – Heat One, *Gonzalez*, 1:48; Heat Two, *Trintignant*,
1:52; Final, *Gonzalez*; FL – Heat One, *Gonzalez*, 2:03, 85.67
mph; Heat Two, *Trintignant*, 1:57, 90.06 mph; Final, *Gonzalez*, 1:50, 95.79 mph

2 May – Gran Premio Bari, I – 60 laps, 206.46 miles
Ferrari 625 *Froilan Gonzalez* 2:21:08.4, 87.80 mph
PP – n/a; FL – Maserati 250F *Onofre Marimon*, 2:16.5,
89.49 mph

**6 June – Gran Premio Roma, Castelfusano, I – 60 laps,
245.69 miles**
Maserati 250F *Onofre Marimon* 2:18:48.6, 106.20 mph
PP – *Marimon*, 2:15.4; FL – *Marimon*, 2:15.7, 108.63 mph

**6 June – GP des Frontières, Chimay, B – 20 laps, 134.54
miles**
Maserati A6GCM/250F *'B. Bira'* 1:22:15.0, 98.19 mph
PP – n/a; FL – Gordini Type 16 *Jacques Pollet*, 3:51.0,
102.17 mph

7 June – Cornwall MRC Formula 1 race, Davidstow, Cornwall, GB – 20 laps, 37.00 miles
Connaught A-Type *John Riseley-Prichard* 29:54.9, 74.21
mph
PP – n/a; FL – *Riseley Prichard*, 1:03.7, 75.92 mph

**7 June – BARC Formula 1 race, Goodwood, GB – 5 laps,
12.00 miles**
Ferrari 625 *Reg Parnell* 8:13.2, 87.60 mph
PP – n/a; FL – Maserati 250F *Roy Salvadori*, 1:35.0, 90.95
mph

**19 June – Crystal Palace Trophy, London, GB – Two 10-lap,
13.90-mile Heats, 10-lap Final, 13.90 miles**
Heat One: Ferrari 625 *Reg Parnell* 11:26.6, 72.94 mph
Heat Two: Cooper-Bristol T20 *Rodney Nuckey* 11:36.4,
71.87 mph
Final: Ferrari 625 *Reg Parnell* 11:26.6, 72.94 mph
PP – Heat One, Connaught A-Type *Peter Collins* time n/a;
Heat Two, Connaught A-Type *Don Beauman* time n/a;
Final, *Parnell*; FL – Heat One, *Parnell*, 1:07, 74.61 mph;
Heat Two, Cooper-Bristol T20 *Rodney Nuckey*, 1:08, 73.59
mph; Final, *Parnell*, 1:07, 74.69 mph

**20 June, BELGIAN GRAND PRIX, Spa-Francorchamps
– 36 laps, 315.47 miles**
Maserati 250F *Juan Fangio* 2:44:42.4, 114.99 mph
PP – *Fangio*, 4:22.1; FL – *Fangio*, 4:25.5, 118.97 mph

**4 July – GRAND PRIX DE L'ACF, Reims-Gueux – 61
laps, 344.76 miles**
Mercedes-Benz W196 *Juan Fangio* 2:42:47.9, 115.98 mph
PP – *Fangio*, 2:29.4; FL – Mercedes-Benz W196 *Hans Herrmann*, 2:32.9, 121.46 mph

**11 July – Grand Prix de Rouen-les-Essarts, F – 95 laps,
302.85 miles**
Ferrari 625 *Maurice Trintignant* 3:40:34.5, 82.37 mph
PP – *Trintignant*, 2:09.4; FL – *Trintignant*, 2:09.9, 88.33
mph

**17 July – BRITISH GRAND PRIX, Silverstone – 90 laps,
263.42 miles**
Ferrari 625 *Froilan Gonzalez* 2:56:14, 89.69 mph
PP – Mercedes-Benz W196 *Juan Fangio*, 1:45; FL – Maserati 250F *Alberto Ascari, Onofre Marimon*, Gordini Type
16 *Jean Behra*, Mercedes-Benz W196 *Mike Hawthorn* and
Gonzalez*, 1:50, 95.79 mph
(*This preposterous multiple fastest lap credit was achieved
by the RAC using egg-timers instead of a more accurate
timing method capable of splitting six times).

**25 July – Grand Prix de Caen, Le Prairie, F – 60 laps,
131.24 miles**
Ferrari 625 *Maurice Trintignant* 1:29:01.1, 88.54 mph
PP – *Trintignant*, 1:26.0; FL – Maserati 250F *Stirling Moss*,
1:25.7, 92.40 mph

**1 August – GERMAN GRAND PRIX, Nürburgring – 22
laps, 312.73 miles**
Mercedes-Benz W196 *Juan Fangio* 3:45:45.8, 83.11 miles
PP – *Fangio*, 9:50.1; FL – Mercedes-Benz W196 *Karl Kling*,
9:55.1, 85.75 mph

**2 August – August Trophy, Crystal Palace, London – Two
10-lap, 13.90-mile Heats, 10-lap Final, 13.90 miles**
Heat One: Ferrari 625 *Reg Parnell* 11:17.9, 73.81 mph
Heat Two: Connaught A-Type *Tony Rolt* 11:47.4, 70.78 mph
Final: Ferrari 625 *Reg Parnell* 11:10.8, 74.59 mph
PP – Heat One, *Parnell* (time n/a); Heat Two, *Rolt* (time
n/a); Final, *Parnell*; FL – Heat One, *Parnell*, 1:06.4, 75.36
mph; Heat Two, Cooper-Bristol T20 *Tony Crook*, 1:09.4,
72.10 mph; Final, *Parnell*, 1:06.0, 75.82 mph

**2 August – Cornwall MRC Formula 1 race, Davidstow, GB
– 20 laps, 37.00 miles**
Lotus MkX *John Coombs* 28:57.8, 76.65 mph
PP – n/a; FL – *Coombs* and Cooper-Bristol T20 *Rodney
Nuckey*, 1:29.5, 74.73 mph

**7 August – International Gold Cup, Oulton Park, GB – 36
laps, 99.40 miles**
Maserati 250F *Stirling Moss* 1:11:27.0, 83.48 mph
PP – Cooper-Bristol T20 *Bob Gerard* 1:59.4*; FL – *Moss*,
1:56.8, 85.11 mph
(*Time set in Moss's absence from practice)

**14 August – RedeX Trophy, Snetterton – 40 laps, 108.40
miles**
Ferrari 625 *Reg Parnell* 1:13:16.8, 88.42 mph
PP – n/a; FL – *Parnell*, 1:48.4, 89.67 mph

15 August – Gran Premio Pescara, I – 16 laps, 255.30 miles
Maserati 250F *Luigi Musso* 2:55:54.51, 86.73 mph
PP – Maserati 250F *Stirling Moss*, 10:23; FL – Maserati 250F *'B. Bira'*, 10:46.39, 88.45 mph

22 August – SWISS GRAND PRIX, Bremgarten, Berne, 66 laps, 240.25 miles
Mercedes-Benz W196 *Juan Fangio* 3:00:34.5, 99.14 mph
PP – Ferrari 625 *Froilan Gonzalez*, 2:39.5; FL – Fangio, 2:39.7, 102.91 mph

28 August – Joe Fry Memorial Trophy, Castle Combe, GB – 15 laps, 27.60 miles
Cooper-Bristol T20 *Horace Gould* 19:49.0, 83.56 mph
PP – n/a; FL – Cooper-Bristol T20 *Bob Gerard*, 1:16.2, 86.93 mph

5 September – ITALIAN GRAND PRIX, Monza – 80 laps, 187.78 miles
Mercedes-Benz W196 *Juan Fangio* 2:47:47.9, 111.91 mph
PP – *Fangio*, 1:59.0; FL – Ferrari 555 *Froilan Gonzalez*, 2:00.8, 116.67 mph

12 September – Circuit de Cadours, F – Two 15-lap, 36.75-mile Heats & Repêchage, 30-lap Final, 74.50 miles
Heat One: Gordini Type 16 *Jean Behra* 30:33, 72.34 mph
Heat Two: Maserati A6GCM/250F *Harry Schell* 31:17, 70.42 mph
Repêchage details n/a
Final: Gordini Type 16 *Jean Behra* 58:49.8, 76.32 mph
PP – n/a; FL n/a

19 September – Grosser Preis von Berlin, AVUS, D – 60 laps, 313.20 miles
Mercedes-Benz W196 *Karl Kling* 2:19:59.8, 132.66 mph
PP – Mercedes-Benz W196 *Juan Fangio*, 2:12.3; FL – *Fangio*, 2:13.4, 137.74 mph

25 September – Goodwood Trophy, GB – 21 laps, 50.40 miles
Maserati 250F *Stirling Moss* 33:03.2, 91.48 mph
PP – *Moss*, 1:32.1; FL – *Moss*, 1:33.0, 92.90 mph

October – 'The Daily Telegraph' Trophy, Aintree – 17 laps, 51.00 miles
Maserati 250F *Stirling Moss* 35:49.0, 85.43 mph
PP – *Moss*, 2:03.6; *Moss* and Vanwall *Mike Hawthorn*, 2:04.8, 86.54 mph

26 October – SPANISH GRAND PRIX, Pedralbes, Barcelona – 80 laps, 313.19 miles
Ferrari 555 *Mike Hawthorn* 3:13:52.1, 97.86 mph
PP – Lancia D50 *Alberto Ascari*, 2:18.1; FL – *Ascari*, 2:20.4, 100.38 mph

1955

16 January – ARGENTINE GRAND PRIX, Buenos Aires – 96 laps, 233.01 miles
Mercedes-Benz W196 *Juan Fangio* 3:00:38.6, 80.57 mph
PP – Ferrari 625 *Froilan Gonzalez*, 1:43.1; FL – *Fangio*, 1:48.3, 80.81 mph

27 March – Gran Premio del Valentino, Valentino Park, Turin, I – 90 laps, 234.81 miles
Lancia D50 *Alberto Ascari* 2:40:21.1, 87.86 mph
PP – *Ascari*, 1:42.0 FL – Maserati 250F *Jean Behra*, 1:43.1, 90.86 mph

11 April – Glover Trophy, Goodwood, GB – 21 laps, 50.40 miles
Maserati 250F *Roy Salvadori* 33:53.0, 89.26 mph
PP – Maserati 250F *Stirling Moss* time n/a; FL – *Salvadori*, 1:33.8, 92.11 mph

11 April – Grand Prix de Pau, F – 110 laps, 188.54 miles
Maserati 250F *Jean Behra* 3:02:09.6, 62.34 mph
PP – Lancia D50 *Alberto Ascari*, 1:34.5; FL – *Ascari*, 66.52 mph

24 April – Grand Prix de Bordeaux, F – 123 laps, 187.85 miles
Maserati 250F *Jean Behra* 2:54:12.6, 65.07 mph
PP – *Behra*, 1:21.7; FL – Maserati 250F *Stirling Moss*, 1:21.3, 67.67 mph

5 June – Curtis Trophy, Snetterton, GB – 10 laps, 27.10 miles
Maserati 250F *Roy Salvadori* 18:26.4, 87.85 mph
PP – n/a; FL – *Salvadori*, 1:49.2, 89.34 mph

6 June – Gran Premio Roma, Castelfufusano 7 May – BRDC International Trophy, Silverstone, GB – 60 laps, 175.61 miles
Maserati 250F *Peter Collins* 1:49:50, 95.94 mph
PP – Maserati 250F *Roy Salvadori*, 1:48; FL – *Collins* and *Salvadori*, 1:47, 98.48 mph

8 May – Gran Premio Napoli, Posillipo, I – 60 laps, 152.86 miles
Lancia D50 *Alberto Ascari* 2:13:03.6, 69.33 mph
PP – *Ascari*, 2:08.1; FL – Maserati 250F *Jean Behra*, 2:09.4, 70.83 mph

22 May – MONACO GRAND PRIX, Monte Carlo – 100 laps, 195.41 miles
Ferrari 625 *Maurice Trintignant* 2:58:09.7, 65.77 mph
PP – Mercedes-Benz W196 *Juan Fangio*, 1:41.1; FL – *Fangio*, 1:42.4, 68.73 mph

29 May – Grand Prix d'Albi, Les Planques, F – 105 laps, 195.09 miles
Maserati 250F *André Simon* 2:23:22.1, 81.66 mph
PP – *Simon*, 1:18.1; FL – *Simon*, 1:17.1, 86.75 mph

29 May – Curtis Trophy, Snetterton, GB – 10 laps, 27.10 miles
Maserati 250F *Roy Salvadori* 18:11.8, 89.03 mph
PP – n/a; FL – *Salvadori*, 1:48.0, 90.00 mph

30 May – Cornwall MRC Formula 1 Race, Davidstow, GB – 20 laps, 37.00 miles
Connaught B-Type *Leslie Marr* time n/a
PP – n/a; FL – n/a

5 June – BELGIAN GRAND PRIX, Spa-Francorchamps – 36 laps, 315.47 miles
Mercedes-Benz W196 *Juan Fangio* 2:39:29.0
PP – Lancia D50 *Eugenio Castellotti*, 4:18.1; FL – *Fangio*, 4:20.6, 121.21 mph

19 June – DUTCH GRAND PRIX, Zandvoort – 100 laps, 260.54 miles
Mercedes-Benz W196 *Juan Fangio* 2:54:23.8, 89.62 mph
PP – *Fangio*, 1:40.0; FL – Maserati 250F *Roberto Mieres*, 1:40.9, 92.96 mph

16 July – BRITISH GRAND PRIX, Aintree – 90 laps, 270.00 miles
Mercedes-Benz W196 *Stirling Moss* 3:07:21.2, 86.47 mph
PP – *Moss*, 2:00.4; FL – *Moss*, 2:00.4, 89.70 mph

30 July – London Trophy, Crystal Palace, London, GB – Two 10-lap, 13.50-mile Heats, two 15-lap Finals, each 20.85 miles
Heat One: Maserati 250F *Mike Hawthorn* 11:00.6, 75.75 mph
Heat Two: Vanwall *Harry Schell* 11:04.4
Consolation Final: Cooper-Bristol T20 *Bob Gerard* 11:13.2, 74.33 mph
Final: Maserati 250F *Mike Hawthorn* 16:10.0, 77.30 mph
PP – Heat One, *Hawthorn*, 1:05.8; Heat Two, *Schell*, 1:04.4; Con. Final, n/a; Final, *Hawthorn*; FL – Heat One, *Hawthorn*, 1:04.2, 77.94 mph; Heat Two, *Schell*, 1:05.2; Con. Final, *Gerard*, 1:05.0, 76.98 mph; Final, *Hawthorn*, 1:03.4, 78.93 mph

6 August – 'The Daily Record' Trophy, Charterhall, Scotland – Two 15-lap, 30.00-mile Heats, 20-lap Final, 40.00 miles
Heat One: Lotus Eleven *Mike Anthony* 23:04.2, 78.02 mph
Heat Two: Maserati 250F *Bob Gerard* 21:26.4, 83.66 mph
Final: Maserati 250F *Bob Gerard* 28:49.0, 83.29 mph
PP – Heats n/a; Final, *Gerard*; FL – Heat One, *Anthony*, 1:30.2, 79.82 mph; Heat Two, *Gerard*, 1:24.0, 85.71 mph; Final, *Gerard* and Maserati 250F *Louis Rosier*, 1:23.5, 85.92 mph

13 August – RedeX Trophy, Snetterton – 25 laps, 67.75 miles
Vanwall *Harry Schell* 50:07.4, 80.80 mph
PP – Maserati 250F *Stirling Moss*, time n/a; FL – *Moss*, 1:56.0, 83.79 mph

3 September – The Daily Telegraph Trophy, Aintree, GB – 17 laps, 51.00 miles
Maserati 250F *Roy Salvadori* 36:33.0, 83.72 mph
PP – Maserati 250F *Stirling Moss* time n/a; FL – *Salvadori*, 2:05.2, 86.26 mph

11 September – ITALIAN GRAND PRIX, Monza – 50 laps, 329.34 miles
Mercedes-Benz W196 *Juan Fangio* 2:25:04.4, 128.50 mph
PP – *Fangio*, 2:46.5; FL – Mercedes-Benz W196 *Stirling Moss*, 2:46.9, 134.04 mph

24 September – International Gold Cup, Oulton Park, GB – 54 laps, 161.09 miles
Maserati 250F *Stirling Moss* 1:44:05.4, 85.94 mph
PP – Lancia D50* *Mike Hawthorn*, 1:52.4; FL – *Moss*, 1:53.2, 87.81 mph
(*Hawthorn was driving a Ferrari-owned and entered ex-Works Lancia D50, soon to form the basis of the 1956 Lancia-Ferrari D50A (*Ameliorata*) models)

1 October – Avon International Trophy, Castle Combe, GB – 55 laps, 101.20 miles
Vanwall *Harry Schell* 1:10.32.8, 86.07 mph
PP – n/a; FL – *Schell*, 1:13.6, 90.00 mph

23 October – Gran Premio Siracusa, Sicily, I – 70 laps, 243.46 miles
Connaught B-Type *Tony Brooks* 2:24:55.7, 99.05 mph
PP – Maserati 250F *Luigi Musso*, 2:03.6; FL – *Brooks*, 2:00.2, 102.36 mph

1956

22 January – ARGENTINE GRAND PRIX, Buenos Aires – 98 laps, 237.85 miles
Lancia-Ferrari D50A *Juan Fangio/Eugenio Castellotti* 3:00:03.7, 79.39 mph
PP – *Fangio*, 1:42.5; FL – *Fangio*, 1:45.3, 82.80 mph

5 February – Gran Premio Çiudad de Buenos Aires, ARG – 60 laps, 156.01 miles
Lancia-Ferrari D50A *Juan Fangio* 1:52:38.9, 83.10 mph
PP – *Fangio*, time n/a; FL – *Fangio*, 1:49.2, 85.72 mph

2 April – Glover Trophy, Goodwood, GB – 32 laps, 76.80 miles
Maserati 250F *Stirling Moss* 48:50.4, 94.35 mph
PP – *Moss*, 1:32.0; FL – *Moss*, 1:30.2, 95.79 mph

15 April Gran Premio Siracusa, Sicily, I – 80 laps, 278.24 miles
Lancia-Ferrari D50A *Juan Fangio* 2:48:59.9, 97.07 mph
PP – *Fangio*, 1:58.0; FL – *Fangio*, 1:59.8, 103.48 mph

21 April – Aintree '200', Liverpool, GB – 67 laps, 201.00 miles
Maserati 250F *Stirling Moss* 2:23:06.4, 82.24 mph
PP – Connaught B-Type *Archie Scott-Brown*, 2:03.8; FL – BRM P25 *Tony Brooks*, 2:04.6, 86.68 mph

5 May – BRDC International Trophy, Silverstone, GB – 60 laps, 175.61 miles
Vanwall *Stirling Moss* 1:44:53, 100.47 mph
PP – Moss, 1:42; FL – Moss and BRM P25 *Mike Hawthorn*, 1:43, 102.30 mph

6 May – Gran Premio Napoli, Posillipo, Naples, I – 60 laps, 152.86 miles
Gordini Type 00 *Robert Manzon* 2:20:43.8, 65.13 mph
PP – Lancia-Ferrari D50A *Eugenio Castellotti*, 2:07.7; FL – Lancia-Ferrari D50A *Luigi Musso*, 2:12.3, 69.36 mph

13 May – MONACO GRAND PRIX, Monte Carlo – 100 laps, 195.41 miles
Maserati 250F *Stirling Moss* 3:00:32.9, 64.94 mph; PP – Lancia-Ferrari D50A *Juan Fangio*, 1:44.0; FL – *Fangio*, 1:44.4, 67.37 mph

3 June – BELGIAN GRAND PRIX, Spa-Francorchamps – 36 laps, 315.47 miles
Lancia-Ferrari D50A *Peter Collins* 2:40:00.3, 118.43 mph; PP – Lancia-Ferrari D50A *Juan Fangio*, 4:09.8; FL – Maserati 250F *Stirling Moss*, 4:14.7, 124.02 mph

24 June – Aintree '100', Liverpool, GB – 34 laps, 102.00 miles
Maserati 250F *Horace Gould* 1:13:39.8, 83.08 mph PP – Connaught B-Type *Archie Scott-Brown*, 2:05.8; FL – *Gould*, 2:06.0, 85.71 mph

1 July – GRAND PRIX DE L'ACF, Reims-Gueux – 61 laps, 314.76 miles
Lancia-Ferrari D50A *Peter Collins* 2:34:23.4, 122.29 mph; PP – *Collins*, 2:23.3; FL – Lancia-Ferrari D50A *Juan Fangio*, 2:25.8, 127.37 mph

14 July – BRITISH GRAND PRIX, Silverstone – 101 laps, 295.62 miles
Lancia-Ferrari D50A *Juan Fangio* 2:59:47.0, 98.65 mph; PP – Maserati 250F *Stirling Moss*, 1:41; FL – *Moss*, 1:43.2, 102.10 mph

22 July – Vanwall Trophy, Snetterton – 15 laps, 40.65 miles
Maserati 250F *Roy Salvadori* 26:24.8, 92.00 mph; PP – *Salvadori* (time n/a); FL – Connaught B-Type *Archie Scott-Brown*, 1:41.4, 95.86 mph

5 August – GERMAN GRAND PRIX, Nürburgring – 22 laps, 311.63 miles
Lancia-Ferrari D50A *Juan Fangio* 3:38:43.7, 85.63 mph; PP – *Fangio*, 9:51.2; FL – *Fangio*, 9:41.6, 87.74 mph

26 August – Grand Prix de Caen, Le Prairie, F – 70 laps, 153.11 miles
Maserati 250F *Harry Schell* 1:54:19.4, 80.11 mph; PP – Maserati 250F *Roy Salvadori?* time n/a; FL – *Salvadori*, 1:26.2, 91.29 mph

2 September – ITALIAN GRAND PRIX, Monza – 50 laps, 310.69 miles
Maserati 250F *Stirling Moss* 2:23:41.3, 129.73 mph; PP – Lancia-Ferrari D50A *Juan Fangio*, 2:32.6; FL – *Moss*, 2:45.5, 135.50 mph

14 October – BRSCC Formula 1 Race, Brands Hatch, GB – 15 laps, 18.60 miles
Connaught B-Type *Archie-Scott-Brown* 15:07.6, 73.78 mph; PP – Connaught B-Type *Stuart Lewis-Evans*, 00:58.8; FL – *Scott-Brown*, 00:59.0, 75.66 mph

1957

13 January – ARGENTINE GRAND PRIX, Buenos Aires – 100 laps, 239.86 miles
Maserati 250F *Juan Fangio* 3:00:55.9, 80.62 mph; PP – Maserati 250F *Stirling Moss*, 1:42.6; FL – *Moss*, 1:44.7, 81.58 mph

27 January – Gran Premio Çiudad de Bueno Aires, ARG – Aggregate of two 30-lap Heats, 170.23 miles
Heat One: Maserati 250F *Juan Fangio* 1:10:59.0, 74.31 mph
Heat Two: Lancia-Ferrari *Luigi Musso/Peter Collins* 1:11:20.6, 73.79 mph
Aggregate: Maserati 250F *Juan Fangio* 2:22:30.3, 74.05 mph; PP – Heat One, *Fangio*, 2:18.2; Heat Two, *Fangio*; FL – Heat One, *Fangio*, 2:19.6, 75.43 mph; Heat Two, Lancia-Ferrari *Peter Collins*, 2:19.6, 75.43 mph

7 April – Gran Premio Siracusa, Sicily, I – 80 laps, 278.24 miles
Lancia-Ferrari *Peter Collins* 2:40:11.9, 102.40 mph; PP – *Collins*, 1:55.5; FL – Vanwall *Stirling Moss*, 1:54.3, 107.64 mph

21 April – Grand Prix de Pau, F – 110 laps, 188.54 miles
Maserati 250F *Jean Behra* 3:00:13.7, 62.80 mph; PP – *Behra*, 1:35.7; FL – *Behra*, 1:35.9, 64.47 mph

22 April – Glover Trophy, Goodwood, GB – 32 laps, 76.80 miles
Connaught B-Type *Stuart Lewis Evans* 50:49.8, 90.66 mph; PP – Vanwall *Stirling Moss*, 1:28.2; FL – Vanwall *Tony Brooks*, 1:29.6, 96.43 mph

28 April – Gran Premio di Napoli, Possillipo, Naples, I – 60 laps, 152.86 miles
Lancia-Ferrari D50A *Peter Collins* 2:10:31.2, 70.27 mph; PP – *Collins*, 2:08.0; FL – Lancia-Ferrari D50A *Mike Hawthorn*, 2:05.6, 73.02 mph

19 May – MONACO GRAND PRIX, Monte Carlo – 105 laps, 205.18 miles
Maserati 250F *Juan Fangio* 3:10:12.8, 64.73 mph; PP – *Fangio*, 1:42.7; FL – *Fangio*, 1:45.6, 66.62 mph

7 July – GRAND PRIX DE L'ACF, Rouen-les-Essarts – 77 laps, 312.24 miles
Maserati 250F *Juan Fangio* 3:26:46.4, 100.20 mph; PP – *Fangio*, 2:21.5; FL – Lancia-Ferrari *Luigi Musso*, 2:22.5, 102.87 mph

14 July – Grand Prix de Reims – Reims-Gueux, F – 61 laps, 314.76 miles
Lancia-Ferrari *Luigi Musso* 2:33:02.6, 123.04 mph; PP – Maserati 250F *Juan Fangio*, 2:23.3; FL – Maserati 250F *Jean Behra*, 2:27.8, 125.70 mph

20 July – BRITISH GRAND PRIX, Aintree – 90 laps, 270.00 miles
Vanwall *Stirling Moss/Tony Brooks* 3:06:37.8, 86.80 mph; PP – *Moss*, 2:00.2; FL – *Moss*, 1:59.2, 90.60 mph

28 July – Grand Prix de Caen, La Prairie, F – 85 laps, 185.92 miles
BRM P25 *Jean Behra* 2:01:35.0, 92.00 mph; PP – *Behra*, 1:21.1; FL – *Behra*, 1:20.7, 97.00 mph

4 August – GERMAN GRAND PRIX, Nürburgring – 22 laps, 311.32 miles
Maserati 250F *Juan Fangio* 3:30:38.3, 88.70 mph; PP – *Fangio*, 9:25.6; FL – *Fangio*, 9:17.4, 91.50 mph

18 August – Gran Premio Pescara, I – 18 laps, 286.11 miles
Vanwall *Stirling Moss* 2:59:22.7, 95.55 mph; PP – Maserati 250F *Juan Fangio*, 9:44.6; FL – *Moss*, 9:44.6, 97.87 mph

8 September – ITALIAN GRAND PRIX, Monza – 87 laps, 310.86 miles
Vanwall *Stirling Moss* 2:35:03.9, 120.28 mph; PP – Vanwall *Stuart Lewis-Evans*, 1:42.4; FL – Vanwall *Tony Brooks*, 1:43.7, 124.04 mph

14 September – BRDC International Trophy, Silverstone, GB – Two 15-lap, 43.90-mile Heats, 35-lap Final, 102.44 miles
Heat One: BRM P25 *Jean Behra* 25:58.8, 101.40 mph
Heat Two: BRM P25 *Harry Schell* 26:58, 97.68 mph
Final: BRM P25 *Jean Behra* 1:01:30, 99.95 mph
PP – Heat One, **REAR-ENGINED Cooper-Climax** T43 *Tony Brooks,* 1:43.0; Heat Two, *Schell*, 1:44.8; Final, *Behra*; FL – Heat One, *Behra*, 1:42, 103.31 mph; Heat Two, n/a; Final, *Behra*, 1:43.0, 102.30 mph

22 September – Gran Premio di Modena, I – Aggregate of two 40-lap Heats, 117.71 miles
Heat One: Maserati 250F *Jean Behra* 42:23.1, 81.14 mph
Heat Two: Maserati 250F *Jean Behra* 42:24.8, 81.01 mph?
Aggregate: Maserati 250F *Jean Behra* 1:24:47.9, 81.09 mph
PP – Heat One, n/a; Heat Two, n/a; FL – Heat One, *Behra* and Ferrari Dino *Luigi Musso*, 1:02.2, 83.04 mph; Heat Two, *Behra*, 1:02.6, 82.41 mph

27 October – Moroccan Grand Prix, Ain-Diab, Casablanca – 55 laps, 261.45 miles
Maserati 250F *Jean Behra* 2:18:23.0, 112.65 mph; PP – Vanwall *Tony Brooks*, 2:23.3; FL – Maserati 250F *Juan Fangio*, 2:25.6

1958

19 January – ARGENTINE GRAND PRIX, Buenos Aires – 80 laps, 167.78 miles
Race won by *Stirling Moss* in Rob Walker's rear-engined Cooper-Climax, the first Post-War Grand Prix victory to fall to a car with its engine "in the wrong end" . . . PP – Maserati 250F *Juan Fangio*, 1:42.0; FL – *Fangio*, 1:41.8, 85.97 mph

7 April – Glover Trophy, Goodwood, GB – 42 laps, 100.80 miles
Ferrari Dino 246 *Mike Hawthorn* 1:03:44.4, 94.96 mph; PP – *Moss*, rear-engined Cooper-Climax; FL – *Hawthorn* and *Moss*, 1:28.8, 97.30 mph

13 April – Gran Premio Siracusa, Sicily, I – 60 laps, 208.68 miles
Ferrari Dino 246 *Luigi Musso* 2:02:44.5, 100.24 mph; PP – *Musso*, 1:58.4; FL – *Musso*, 1:59.1, 103.30 mph

19 April – Aintree '200', Liverpool, GB – 67 laps, 201.00 miles won by Moss in rear-engined Copper Climax.
PP – *Moss*; FL – *Jack Brabham in* rear-engined Cooper-Climax

3 May – BRDC International Trophy, Silverstone, GB – 50 laps, 146.35 miles
Ferrari Dino 246 *Peter Collins* 1:26:14.6, 101.82 mph; PP – *Roy Salvadori* in *rear-engined* Cooper-Climax; FL – n/a

18 June – MONACO GRAND PRIX, Monte Carlo – 100 laps, 195.41 miles
Won by *Maurice Trintignant rear-engined* Cooper-Climax PP – Vanwall *Tony Brooks*, 1:39.8; FL – Ferrari Dino 246 *Mike Hawthorn*, 1:40.6, 69.94 mph

26 June – DUTCH GRAND PRIX, Zandvoort – 75 laps, 195.41 miles
Vanwall *Stirling Moss* 2:04:49.2, 93.90 mph; PP – Vanwall *Stuart Lewis-Evans*, 1:37.1; FL – *Moss*, 1:38.5, 94.78 mph

15 June – BELGIAN GRAND PRIX – 24 laps, 210.31 miles
Vanwall *Tony Brooks* 1:37:06.3, 129.93 mph; PP – Ferrari Dino 246 *Mike Hawthorn*, 3:57.1; FL – *Hawthorn*, 3:58.3, 132.36 mph

6 July – GRAND PRIX DE L'ACF, Reims-Gueux – 50 laps, 258.00 miles
Ferrari Dino 246 *Mike Hawthorn* 2:03:21.3, 125.46 mph; PP – *Hawthorn*, 2:21.7; FL – *Hawthorn*, 2:24.9, 128.17 mph

19 July – BRITISH GRAND PRIX, Silverstone – 75 laps, 219.52 miles
Ferrari Dino 246 *Peter Collins* 2:09:04.2, 102.05 mph; PP – Vanwall *Stirling Moss*, 1:39.4; FL – Ferrari Dino 246 *Mike Hawthorn*, 1:40.8, 104.54 mph

20 July – Grand Prix de Caen, La Prairie, F – 86 laps, 188.11 miles
Won by *Moss* in *rear-engined* Cooper-Climax PP – *Moss*; FL – BRM P25 *Jean Behra*, 1:20.8, 97.43 mph

3 August – GERMAN GRAND PRIX, Nürburgring – 15 laps, 212.48 miles
Vanwall *Tony Brooks* 2:21:15.0, 90.35 mph; PP – Ferrari Dino 246 *Mike Hawthorn*, 9:14.0; FL – Vanwall *Stirling Moss*, 9:09.2, 92.90 mph

24 August – PORTUGUESE GRAND PRIX, Oporto – 50 laps, 230.14 miles
Vanwall *Stirling Moss* 2:11:27.8, 105.03 mph; PP – *Moss*, 2:34.21; FL – Ferrari Dino 246 *Mike Hawthorn*, 2:32.37, 110.75 mph

7 September – ITALIAN GRAND PRIX, Monza – 70 laps, 250.11 miles
Vanwall *Tony Brooks* 2:03:47.8, 121.20 mph; PP – Vanwall *Stirling Moss*, 1:40.5; FL – Ferrari Dino 256 *Phil Hill*, 1:42.9, 125.00 mph

19 October – MOROCCAN GRAND PRIX, Ain-Diab, Casablanca – 55 laps, 261.61 miles
Vanwall *Stirling Moss* 2:09:15.0, 116.20 mph; PP – Ferrari Dino 246 *Mike Hawthorn*, 2:23.1; FL – *Moss*, 2:22.5, 117.80 mph

1959

30 March – Glover Trophy, Goodwood, GB – 42 laps, 100.80 miles
Won by Moss in *rear-engined* Cooper-Climax
PP – BRM P25 *Harry Schell*, 1:39.0; FL – *Moss*

18 April – Aintree '200', Liverpool, GB – 67 laps, 201.00 miles
Ferrari Dino 246/59 *Jean Behra* 2:15:52.0, 88.76 mph; PP – *Masten Gregory's* rear-engined Cooper-Climax; FL – *Moss'* rear-engined Cooper

2 May – BRDC International Trophy, Silverstone – 50 laps, 146.35 miles
Won by *Jack Brabham* in *rear-engined* Cooper-Climax
PP – BRM P25 *Stirling Moss*, 1:39.2; FL – Aston Martin DBR4/250 *Roy Salvadori*, 1:40.0, 105.37 mph

10 May – MONACO GRAND PRIX, Monte Carlo – 100 laps, 195.41 miles
Won by *Brabham's* rear engined Cooper-Climax
PP – *Moss'* rear-engined Cooper-Climax; FL – *Brabham's* Cooper

31 May – DUTCH GRAND PRIX, Zandvoort – 75 laps, 195.41 miles
BRM P25 *Jo Bonnier* 2:05:26.8, 93.46 mph; PP – *Bonnier*, 1:36.0; FL – *Moss'* rear-engined Cooper-Climax, 1:36.6, 97.19 mph

5 July – GRAND PRIX DE L'ACF, Reims-Gueux – 50-laps, 258.00 miles
Ferrari Dino 256 *Tony Brooks* 2:01:26.5, 127.44 mph; PP – *Brooks*, 2:19.4; FL – BRM P25 *Stirling Moss*, 2:22.8, 130.21 mph

18 July – BRITISH GRAND PRIX, Aintree – 75 laps, 225.00 miles
Won by *Brabham's rear-engined* Cooper-Climax; PP – *Brabham*; FL – BRM P25 *Stirling Moss* and *Bruce McLaren's rear-engined* Cooper-Climax, 1:57.0, 92.31 mph

2 August – GERMAN GRAND PRIX, AVUS, Berlin – Aggregate of two 30-lap Heats, 309.46 miles
Heat One: Ferrari Dino 246 *Tony Brooks* 1:03:17.6, 141.83 mph;
Heat Two: Ferrari Dino 246 *Tony Brooks* 1:06:14.0, 134.97 mph;
Aggregate: Ferrari Dino 246 *Tony Brooks* 2:09:31.6, 138.40 mph;
PP – Heat One: *Brooks*, 2:05.9; Heat Two, *Brooks*; FL – Heat One, *Brooks*, 2:04.5, 149.14 mph; Heat Two, Ferrari Dino 246 *Phil Hill*, 2:05.3, 148.21 mph

23 August – PORTUGUESE GRAND PRIX, Monsanto Park, Lisbon – in this race, for the first time, front-engined cars failed to achieve any of the premier performances (Race Win, Pole Position and Fastest Lap) – all went to Moss in rear-engined Cooper-Climax

13 September – ITALIAN GRAND PRIX, Monza – 72 laps, 257.26 miles
Won by *Moss* in *rear-engined* Cooper-Climax; PP – *Moss*; FL – Ferrari Dino 256 *Phil Hill*, 1:40.4, 128.13 mph

26 September – International Gold Cup, Oulton Park, GB – All premier performances by *Moss'* Cooper-Climax

10 October – Silver City Trophy, Snetterton, GB – 25 laps, 67.75 miles
BRM P25 *Ron Flockhart* 39:58.0, 101.71 mph; PP – *Flockhart*, 1:34.8; FL – *Flockhart*, 1:33.6, 103.85 mph

12 December – UNITED STATES GRAND PRIX, Hendrick Field, Sebring, Fla. – All premier performances achieved by rear-engined Cooper-Climax cars

1960

Premier Performances (ie Race Win, Pole Position and Fastest Lap) were all set by rear-engined cars in the following races:

6 February	ARGENTINE GRAND PRIX
18 April	Glover Trophy, Goodwood, GB
14 May	BRDC International Trophy, Silverstone, GB
29 May	MONACO GRAND PRIX, Monte Carlo
6 June	DUTCH GRAND PRIX, Zandvoort
19 June	BELGIAN GRAND PRIX, Spa-Francorchamps
3 July	GRAND PRIX DE L'ACF, Reims-Gueux
16 July	BRITISH GRAND PRIX, Silverstone, GB
1 August	Silver City Trophy, Brands Hatch, GB
14 August	PORTUGUESE GRAND PRIX, Oporto

UNTIL...

**4 September   ITALIAN GRAND PRIX, Monza –
50 laps, 310.69 miles**
Ferrari Dino 246/60 *Phil Hill* 2:21:09.2, 132.07 mph; PP
– *Hill*, 2:41.4; FL – *Hill*, 2:43.6, 136.64 mph
**Making these the last-ever World Championship-qualifying
Grand Prix victory, pole position and fastest lap to be
achieved by a front-engined Formula 1 car...
Rear-engined cars then dominated the closing events of this
1960 Formula 1 season, as follows:**

17 September   Lombank Trophy, Snetterton, GB

24 September   International Gold Cup, GB

**20 November   UNITED STATES GRAND PRIX,
Riverside, California**

1961

**No front-engined car produced any premier performances
until;**

**23 September   International Gold Cup, Oulton Park,
GB – 60 laps, 165.66 miles**
Ferguson-Climax P99 4WD *Stirling Moss* 1:51:53.8, 88.83
mph; PP – Bruce McLaren's *rear-engined* Cooper; FL –
Moss, 1:46.4, 93.42 mph

**These were respectively the last Formula 1 race win and
last Formula 1 fastest lap ever to be set by a car with its
engine ahead of the driver...**

APPENDIX 2

FORMULA 2, 1952-1953 and 1956-1959

During the two seasons of 1952 and 1953, as the contemporary Formula 1 lay down and died for lack of competitive support, 2-litre unsupercharged Formula 2 racing achieved World Championship status. The premier performances achieved in all Formula 2 races during these two seasons, were as follows:

1952

16 March – Gran Premio Siracusa, Sicily, I – 60 laps, 201.32 miles
Ferrari 500 *Alberto Ascari* 2:16:24, 88.36 mph; PP – n/a; FL – Ferrari 500 *Luigi Villoresi*, 2:13, 90.62 mph

14 April – Grand Prix de Pau, F – 3 Hours duration
Ferrari 500 *Alberto Ascari* 99 laps, 169.82 miles, 56.48 mph; PP – *Ascari*, 1:43.3; FL – *Ascari*, 1:44.4, 59.30 mph

14 April – Lavant Cup, Goodwood, GB – 6 laps, 14.40 miles
Cooper-Bristol T20 *Mike Hawthorn* 10:23.1, 83.18 mph; PP – *Hawthorn* (time n/a); FL – *Hawthorn*, 1:42, 84.70 mph

19 April – Ibsley Formula 2 Race, Ibsley Aerodrome, Hampshire, GB – 15 laps, 31.80 miles
Cooper-Bristol T20 *Mike Hawthorn* 25:03.0, 76.17 mph; PP – HWM *George Abecassis*, time n/a; FL – *Hawthorn*, 1:38.4, 77.56 mph

27 April – Circuit de la Ville de Marseilles, F – 3 Hours duration
Ferrari 500 *Alberto Ascari* 134 laps, 223.29 miles, 74.43 mph; PP – *Ascari*, 1:17.8; FL – Ferrari 500 *Dr Giuseppe Farina*, 1:15.4, 77.99 mph

3 May – AMOC Formula 2 Race, Snetterton, GB – 10 laps, 27.10 miles
Frazer Nash *Dickie Stoop* 22:22.8, 72.40 mph; PP – n/a; FL – BMW 328 *Charles Bulmer*, 2:04.8, 77.92 mph

10 May – BRDC International Trophy, Silverstone, GB – Two 15-lap, 43.32-mile Heats, 35-lap Final, 101.08 miles
Heat One: Cooper-Bristol T20 *Mike Hawthorn* 30:49.0, 85.48 mph;
Heat Two: Gordini Type 16 *Robert Manzon* 30:37.0, 86.04 mph;
Final: HWM *Lance Macklin* 1:11:589, 85.41 mph; PP – Heat One, *Hawthorn* and Gordini *Jean Behra*, 2:00, 87.81 mph; Heat Two, Ferrari 500 *Rudi Fischer*, 1:58, 89.28 mph; Final, Ferrari 166 *Peter Whitehead* and *Hawthorn*, 1:59, 88.55 mph

11 May – Gran Premio di Napoli, Possillipo, Naples, I – 60 laps, 152.86 miles
Ferrari 500 *Dr Giuseppe Farina* 2:19:40.4, 65.51 mph; PP – n/a; FL -*Farina*, 2:15.1, 67.74 mph

18 May – SWISS GRAND PRIX, Bremgarten, Berne – 62 laps, 280.24 miles
Ferrari 500 *Piero Taruffi* 3:01:46.1, 92.59 mph; PP – Ferrari 500 *Dr Giuseppe Farina*, 2:47.5; FL – *Taruffi*, 2:49.1, 96.09 mph

25 May – ADAC Eifelrennen, Nürburgring, D – 7 laps, 99.16 miles
Ferrari 500 *Rudi Fischer* 1:16:58.3, 77.25 mph; PP – n/a; FL – *Fischer*, 10:51, 78.37 mph

25 May – Prix de Paris, Montlhéry, F – 3 hours duration
Ferrari 500 *Piero Taruffi* 74 laps, 285.85 miles, 95.28 mph; PP – n/a; FL – *Taruffi*, 2:21.2, 99.54 mph

1 June – Grand Prix des Frontières, Chimay, B – 22 laps, 147.62 miles
HWM *Paul Frère* 1:38:48.0, 90.15 mph; PP – n/a; FL – *Frère*, 4:16.0, 94.92 mph

8 June – Gran Premio dell'Autodromo, Monza, Milan, I – Aggregate of two 35-lap Heats, 274.04 miles
Heat One: Ferrari 500 *Alberto Ascari* 1:15:12.0, 109.32 mph;
Heat Two: Ferrari 500 *Dr Giuseppe Farina* 1:14:58.4, 109.65 mph;
Aggregate: Ferrari 500 *Dr Giuseppe Farina* 2:31:15.0, 108.71 mph;
PP – n/a; FL – Heat One, *Ascari*, 2:05.3, 112.45 mph; Heat Two, *Farina*, 2:06.4, 111.43 mph

8 June – Circuit des Aix-les-Bains, F – Aggregate of two 40-lap Heats, 122.08 miles
Heat One: Gordini Type 16 *Jean Behra* time n/a;
Heat Two: Gordini Type 16 *Jean Behra* time n/a;
Aggregate: Gordini Type 16 *Jean Behra* 2:10:42.1, 55.75 mph; PP – n/a; FL – n/a

21 June – West Essex CC Formula 2 Race, Boreham Aerodrome, GB – 10 laps, 30.00 miles
Cooper-Bristol T20 *Reg Parnell* 20:05.0, 89.62 mph; PP – Connaught A-Type *Ken Downing* time n/a; FL – *Parnell*, 1:58, 91.35 mph

22 June – BELGIAN GRAND PRIX, Spa-Francorchamps – 36 laps, 314.72 miles
Ferrari 500 *Alberto Ascari* 3:03:46.8, 102.90 mph; PP – *Ascari*, 4:37.0; FL – *Ascari*, 4:54, 106.83 mph

29 June – Grand Prix de la Marne, Reims-Gueux, F – 3 hours duration
Gordini Type 16 *Jean Behra* 71 laps, 316.77 miles, 105.33 mph; PP – Ferrari 500 *Alberto Ascari*, 2:26.2; FL – *Ascari*, 2:28.2, 108.37 mph

6 July – GRAND PRIX DE L'ACF, Rouen-les-Essarts – 3 hours duration
Ferrari 500 *Alberto Ascari* 76 laps, 240.20 miles, 80.08 mph; PP – *Ascari*, 2:14.8; FL – *Ascari*, 2:17.3, 82.68 mph

13 July – Grand Prix des Sables d'Olonne, F – 3 hours duration
Ferrari 500 *Luigi Villoresi* 136 laps, 198.45 miles, 76.20 mph; PP – Ferrari 500 *Alberto Ascari*, 1:13; FL – *Ascari*, 1:12.3, 72.75 mph

19 July – BRITISH GRAND PRIX, Silverstone – 85 laps, 248.79 miles
Ferrari 500 *Alberto Ascari* 2:44:11, 90.92 mph; PP – Ferrari 500 *Dr Giuseppe Farina*, 1:50; FL – *Ascari*, 1:52, 94.08 mph

27 July – Grand Prix de Caen, La Prairie, F – 75 laps, 192.10 miles
Gordini Type 16 *Maurice Trintignant* 2:15:34.4, 85.04 mph; PP – n/a; FL – n/a

3 August – GERMAN GRAND PRIX, Nürburgring – 18 laps, 254.88 miles
Ferrari 500 *Alberto Ascari* 3:06:13.3, 82.09 mph; PP – *Ascari*, 10:04.9; FL – *Ascari*, 10:05.1, 84.33 mph

10 August – Grand Prix du Comminges, F – 3 hours duration
Ferrari 500 *Alberto Ascari/André Simon* 95 laps, 258.7 miles, 86.05 mph; PP – *Ascari*, time n/a; FL – *Ascari*, 1:51.2, 88.36 mph

17 August – DUTCH GRAND PRIX, Zandvoort – 90 laps, 234.33 miles
Ferrari 500 *Alberto Ascari* 2:53:28.5, 80.95 mph; PP – *Ascari*, 1:46.5; FL – *Ascari*, 1:49.8

23 August – National Trophy, Turnberry, Scotland – 15 laps, 26.40 miles
Connaught A-Type *Mike Hawthorn* 20:09.0, 78.53 mph; PP – *Hawthorn*, 1:20; FL – n/a

24 August – Grand Prix de la Baule, F – 3 hours duration
Ferrari 500 *Alberto Ascari* 87 laps, 230.7 miles, 76.73 mph; PP – n/a; FL – Ferrari 500 *Luigi Villoresi*, 2:01.1, 79.10 mph

31 August – Grenzlandringrennen, Rheydt, Holland – 12 laps, 67.15 miles
Veritas-BMW *Toni Ulmen* 31:22.1, 128.50 mph; PP – n/a; FL – *Ulmen*, 2:31.4, 132.95 mph

7 September – ITALIAN GRAND PRIX, Monza – 80 laps, 312.76 miles
Ferrari 500 *Alberto Ascari* 2:50:45.6, 112.09 mph; PP – *Ascari*, 2:05.7; FL – *Ascari* and Maserati A6GCM *Froilan Gonzalez*, 2:06.1, 116.61 mph

14 September – Gran Premio di Modena, I – 100 laps, 236.13 miles
Ferrari 500 *Luigi Villoresi* 1:51:21.0, 77.04 mph; PP – Ferrari 500 *Alberto Ascari*, 1:04.4; FL – Maserati A6GCM *Froilan Gonzalez* and *Villoresi*, 1:05.0, 79.43 mph

14 September – Circuit de Cadours, F – Two 15-lap Heats, 10-lap Repêchage, 30-lap Final, 103.20 miles
Heat One: Ferrari 500 *Louis Rosier* 30:55, 73.05 mph;
Heat Two: Gordini Type 16 *Harry Schell* 31:17, 72.26 mph;
Repêchage: HWM *Tony Gaze* 21:41.0, 69.50 mph;
Final: Ferrari 500 *Louis Rosier* 1:01:42, 72.64 mph; PP – n/a; FL – (overall) *Schell*, 2:00, 74.70 mph

27 September – Madgwick Cup, Goodwood, GB – 7 laps, 16.80 miles
Connaught A-Type *Ken Downing* 11:53.0, 84.80 mph; PP – Connaught A-Type *Eric Thompson* time n/a; FL – Connaught A-Type *Dennis Poore*, 1:39.6, 86.75 mph

28 September – Internationales AVUSRennen, Berlin, D – 25 laps, 128.65 miles
Ferrari 500 *Rudi Fischer* 1:06:43.8, 115.69 mph; PP – n/a; FL – *Fischer*, 2:36.5, 118.36 mph

4 October – Joe Fry Memorial Trophy, Castle Combem GB – 20 laps, 36.80 miles
Ferrari 500 *Roy Salvadori* 26:32.6, 83.30 mph; PP – ERA G-Type *Stirling Moss*, 1:18.4; FL – *Salvadori*, 1:17.6, 85.38 mph

11 October – 'The Newcastle Journal' Trophy, Charterhall, Scotland – 40 laps, 80.00 miles
Connaught A-Type *Dennis Poore* 59:21.6, 80.89 mph; PP – n/a; FL – HWM *Tony Gaze*, 1:26.6, 83.72 mph

1953

18 January – ARGENTINE GRAND PRIX, Buenos Aires – 3 hours duration
Ferrari 500 *Alberto Ascari* 3:01:04.6, 97 laps, 77.76 mph; PP – *Ascari*, 1:55.4; FL – *Ascari*, 1:48.4, 80.35 mph

22 March – Gran Premio Siracusa, Sicily, I – 80 laps, 268.40 miles
Maserati A6GCM *Baron Emmanuel de Graffenried* 2:57:31, 92.02 mph; PP – n/a; FL – Ferrari 500 *Alberto Ascari*, 2:05, 98.21 mph

6 April – Lavant Cup, Goodwood, GB 7 laps, 16.80 miles
Maserati A6GCM *Baron Emmanuel de Graffenried* 11:30.6, 87.63 mph; PP – Connaught A-Type *Roy Salvadori*, time n/a; FL – *Salvadori*, 1:36.6, 89.44 mph

6 April – Grand Prix de Pau, F – 3 hours duration
Ferrari 500 *Alberto Ascari* 106 laps, 181.81 miles, 60.47 mph; PP – *Ascari*, 1:39.2; FL – *Ascari*, 1:38.9, 62.49 mph

18 April – AMOC Formula 1 Race, Snetterton, GB – 10 laps, 27.10 miles
Connaught A-Type *Eric Thompson* 19:11.0, 84.44 mph; PP – n/a; FL – *Thompson*, 1:49.0, 89.44 mph

3 May – AMOC Spring Trophy, Snetterton, GB – 10 laps, 27.10 miles
Frazer Nash *Eric Thompson* 22:17.5, 72.40 mph; PP – n/a; FL – n/a

3 May – Grand Prix de Bordeaux, F – 120 laps, 183.12 miles
Ferrari 500 *Alberto Ascari* 2:58:59.5, 62.83 mph; PP – n/a; FL – Ferrari 500 *Dr Giuseppe Farina*, 1:24.6, 64.845 mph

9 May – BRDC International Trophy, Silverstone, GB – Two 15-lap, 43.32-mile Heats, 35-lap Final, 101.08 miles
Heat One: Maserati A6GCM *Baron Emmanuel de Graffenried* 28:50, 90.89 mph;
Heat Two: Ferrari 500 *Mike Hawthorn* 28:23, 92.81 mph
Final: Ferrari 500 *Mike Hawthorn* 1:06:36, 92.29 mph
PP – Heat One, *de Graffenried*, 1:51; Heat Two, Cooper-Bristol T23 *Ken Wharton*, 1:52; Final, *Hawthorn*; FL – Heat One, *de Graffenried* and Cooper-Alta *Stirling Moss*, 1:54, 92.43 mph; Heat Two, *Hawthorn*, 1:51, 94.93 mph; Final, *Hawthorn* and *de Graffenried*, 1:51?, 94.93 mph

10 May – Gran Premio di Napoli, Possillipo, Naples, I – 60 laps, 152.86 miles
Ferrari 500 *Dr Giuseppe Farina* 2:12:17.5, 69.28 mph; PP – n/a; FL – Ferrari 500 *Alberto Ascari*, 2:07.8, 71.77 mph

16 May – Ulster Trophy, Dundrod, NI – Two 10-lap, 74.16-mile Heats, 14-lap Final, 103.82 miles
Heat One: HWM *Duncan Hamilton* 52.32, 84.70 mph
Heat Two: Ferrari 500 *Mike Hawthorn* 50:24, 88.28 mph
Final: Ferrari 500 *Mike Hawthorn* 1:12:01.6, 86.49 mph;
PP – Heat One, Connaught A-Type *Stirling Moss*, 4:59; Heat Two, *Hawthorn* 4:51; Final, *Hawthorn*; FL – Heat One, *Moss*, 4:56, 90.19 mph; Heat Two: *Hawthorn*, 4:54, 90.81 mph; Final, *Hawthorn*, 5:00, 88.99 mph

24 May – Grand Prix des Frontières, Chimay, B – 20 laps, 134.54 miles
Gordini Type 16 *Maurice Trintignant* 1:25:59.5, 94.06 mph; PP – n/a; FL – *Trintignant*, 4:10.5, 96.66 mph

25 May – Coronation Trophy, Crystal Palace, London, GB – Two 10-lap Heats and Final, each 13.50 miles
Heat One: Connaught A-Type *Tony Rolt* 11:47.4, 70.78 mph
Heat Two: Cooper-Bristol T23 *Peter Whitehead* 12:00.8, 69.40 mph
Final: Connaught A-Type *Tony Rolt* 11:42.2, 71.28 mph
PP – Heat One, *Rolt*, time n/a; Heat Two, *Whitehead*, time n/a; Final, *Rolt*: FL – Heat One, *Rolt*, 1:08.8, 72.73 mph; Heat Two, *Whitehead*, 1:08.6, 70.88 mph; Final, *Rolt*, 1:08.8, 72.73 mph

30 May – Coronation Formula 2 Race, Snetterton, GB – 10 laps, 27.10 miles
Connaught A-Type *Tony Rolt* 18:55.8, 85.58 mph; PP – ??; FL – *Rolt*, 1:51.6, 87.08 mph

31 May – ADAC Eifelrennen, Nürburgring, D – 7 laps, 95.86 miles
Maserati A6GCM *Baron Emmanuel de Graffenried* 1:24:32.0, 70.36 mph; PP – n/a; FL – *de Graffenried*, 11:24.3, 72.04 mph

7 June – DUTCH GRAND PRIX, Zandvoort – 90 laps, 234.33 miles
Ferrari 500 *Alberto Ascari* 2:53:35.8, 80.99 mph; PP – *Ascari*, 1:51.1; FL – Ferrari 500 *Luigi Villoresi*, 1:52.8, 83.10 mph

21 June – BELGIAN GRAND PRIX, Spa-Francorchamps – 36 laps, 314.72 miles
Ferrari 500 *Alberto Ascari* 2:48:30.3, 112.47 mph; PP – Maserati A6GCM *Juan Fangio*, 4:30; FL – Maserati A6GCM *Froilan Gonzalez*, 4:34, 115.52 mph

27 June – West Essex CC Formula 2 Race, Snetterton, GB – 10 laps, 27.10 miles
Connaught A-Type *Kenneth McAlpine* 18:53.4, 85.76 mph; PP – n/a; FL – Connaught A-Type *Roy Salvadori*, 1:51.2, 87.41 mph

27 June – MMEC Formula 2 Race, Silverstone, GB – 6 laps, 9.64 miles
Cooper-Alta *Tony Crook* 7:34.3, 76.41 mph; PP – n/a; FL – n/a

5 July – GRAND PRIX DE L'ACF, Reims-Gueux – 60 laps, 311.23 miles
Ferrari 500 *Mike Hawthorn* 2:44:18.6, 113.65 mph; PP – Ferrari 500 *Alberto Ascari*, 2:41.2; FL – Maserati A6GCM *Juan Fangio*, 2:41.1, 115.91 mph

11 July – Crystal Palace Trophy, London, GB – 15 laps, 20.85 miles
Connaught A-Type *Tony Rolt* 17:23.4, 71.94 mph; PP – *Rolt*, time n/a; FL – n/a

12 July – Internationales AVUSRennen, Berlin, D – 25 laps, 128.65 miles
Ferrari 500 *Jacques Swaters* 1:05:03.3, 117.60 mph; PP – n/a; FL – Veritas-BMW *Theo Helfrich*, 2:34.1, 120.20 mph

18 July – BRITISH GRAND PRIX, Silverstone – 90 laps, 263.42 miles
Ferrari 500 *Alberto Ascari* 2:50:00, 92.97 mph; PP – *Ascari*, 1:48; FL – *Ascari* and Maserati A6GCM *Froilan Gonzalez*, 1:50, 95.79 mph

25 July – USAF Trophy, Snetterton, GB – 15 laps, 40.65 miles
Connaught A-Type *Tony Rolt* 28:21.2, 85.70 mph; PP – n/a; FL – Cooper-Bristol T23 *Bob Gerard*, 1:51.4, 87.25 mph

26 July – Circuit des Aix-les-Bains, F – Aggregate of two 50-lap Heats, 149.70 miles
Heat One: Gordini Type 16 *Jean Behra* 1:11:33.8, 62.78 mph;
Heat Two: OSCA *Elie Bayol* 1:10:48.9, 63.42 mph;
Aggregate: OSCA *Elie Bayol* 2:22:45.4, 62.04 mph
PP – n/a; FL – Heat One, Gordini Type 16 *Harry Schell*, 1:20.3, 66.3 mph; Heat Two, *Behra*, 1:20.0, 66.65 mph

2 August – GERMAN GRAND PRIX, Nürburgring – 18 laps, 254.88 miles
Ferrari 500 *Dr Giuseppe Farina* 3:02:25.0, 83.89 mph; PP – *Ascari*, 9:59.8; FL – *Ascari*, 9:56.0, 85.62 mph

3 August – Thruxton Formula 2 Race, Hampshire, GB – 20 laps, 55.00 miles
Connaught A-Type *Tony Rolt* 41:15, 80.21 mph; PP – n/a; FL – *Rolt*, 2:00, 82.72 mph

9 August – Grand Prix des Sables d'Olonne, F – Aggregate of two 45-lap Heats, 245.60 miles
Heat One: Gordini Type 16 *Jean Behra* time n/a
Heat Two: Gordini Type 16 *Maurice Trintignant* time n/a
Aggregate: Ferrari 500 *Louis Rosier** 2:12:56.1, 74.42 mph;
PP n/a; FL – n/a
(*Rosier finished 3rd in Heat One and 2nd in Heat Two)

15 August – 'The Newcastle Journal' Trophy, Charterhall, Scotland – 50 laps, 100.00 miles
Cooper-Bristol T23 *Ken Wharton* 1:15:30.6, 79.45 mph; PP – n/a; FL – *Wharton* and Connaught A-Types *Roy Salvadori* and *Ron Flockhart*, 1:26.0, 83.70 mph

23 August – SWISS GRAND PRIX, Bremgarten, Berne, 65 laps, 293.54 miles
Ferrari 500 *Alberto Ascari* 3:01:34.40, 97.10 mph; PP – Maserati A6GCM *Juan Fangio*, 2:40.1; FL – *Ascari*, 2:41.3, 100.46 mph

30 August – Circuit de Cadours, F – Two 15-lap, 38.25-mile Heats, 10-lap, 25.50-mile Repêchage, 30-lap Final, 76.50 miles
Heat One: Gordini Type 16 *Maurice Trintignant* 30:55, 74.23 mph;
Heat Two: Gordini Type 16 *Harry Schell* 30:50, 74.43 mph
Repêchage: n/a
Final: Gordini Type 16 *Maurice Trintignant* 1:00:52, 75.41 mph;
PP – n/a; FL – (overall) *Trintignant*, 1:56, 77.10 mph

12 September – RedeX Trophy, Snetterton, GB – 10 laps, 27.10 miles
Connaught A-Type *Eric Thompson* 19:00.0, 85.26 mph; PP – n/a; FL – *Thompson*, 1:52.6, 86.32 mph

13 September – ITALIAN GRAND PRIX, Monza – 80 laps, 313.20 miles
Maserati A6GCM *Juan Fangio* 2:49:45.9, 110.62 mph; PP – *Ascari*, 2:02.7; FL – *Fangio*, 2:04.6, 113.13 mph

19 September – London Trophy, Crystal Palace, GB – Aggregate of two 10-lap Heats, 27.00 miles
Heat One: Cooper-Alta *Stirling Moss* 11:48.0, 70.68 mph
Heat Two: Cooper-Alta *Stirling Moss* 11:36.4, 71.86 mph
Aggregate: Cooper-Alta *Stirling Moss* 23:24.2, 71.27 mph
PP – Heat One, *Moss*, time n/a; Heat Two, *Moss*, time n/a; FL – (overall) Connaught A-Type *Ron Flockhart*, 1:08.0, 73.59 mph

20 September – Gran Premio di Modena, I – 100 laps, 236.13 miles
Maserati A6GCM *Juan Fangio* 1:52:08.9, 76.62 mph; PP – Maserati A6GCM *Baron Emmanuel de Graffenried*, time n/a; FL – *Fangio*, 1:05.4, 78.83 mph

26 September – Madgwick Cup, Goodwood, GB – 7 laps, 16.80 miles
Connaught A-Type *Roy Salvadori* 11:15.0, 89.63 mph; PP – *Salvadori*, time n/a; FL – *Salvadori*, 1:35.0, 90.95 mph

3 October – Joe Fry Memorial Trophy, Castle Combe, GB – 20 laps, 36.81 miles
Cooper-Bristol *Bob Gerard* 25:56.2, 85.14 mph; PP – n/a; FL – *Gerard*, 1:16.2, 86.92 mph

8 October – Oulton Park Formula 2 Race, GB – 33 laps, 49.63 miles
Connaught A-Type *Tony Rolt* 38:33.4, 77.26 mph; PP – Cooper-JAP *Les Leston*, 1:09.0; FL – *Rolt*, 1:08.2, 79.41 mph

17 October – Curtis Trophy, Snetterton, GB – 15 laps, 40.65 miles
Cooper-Bristol *Bob Gerard* 33:45.0, 72.27 mph; PP – n/a; FL – *Gerard*, 2:08.8, 75.74 mph

Hereafter Formula 2 lapsed until a new 1500cc class was introduced in Britain during 1956, which then became internationally-accepted from 1957-1960. Front-engined cars provided premier performances in the following events:

1956

14 July – British Grand Prix meeting, Formula 2 race, Silverstone – 25 laps, 73.17 miles
Won by *Roy Salvadori's* rear-engined Cooper-Climax; PP – *Salvadori*, 1:49; FL – Lotus-Climax 11* *Colin Chapman*, 1:47.6, 97.93 mph
(*This car was a Lotus 11 sports car, stripped of its lights, generator etc, for use under Formula 2 regulations)

6 August – BRSCC Bank Holiday F2 Race, Brands Hatch, GB – 16 laps, 19.84 miles
Won by *Salvadori's* Cooper-Climax; PP – Lotus-Climax 11 *Colin Chapman*, FL – Lotus-Climax 11 *Reg Bicknell*, 1:01.0, 73.18 mph

9 September – BRSCC Formula 2 Race, Brands Hatch, GB – 15 laps, 18.60 miles
Lotus-Climax 11 *Colin Chapman* 15:57.2, 70.40 mph; PP – *Dennis Taylor's* rear-engined Cooper-Climax; FL – *Chapman*, 1:02.2, 71.77 mph

1957

Rear-engined cars dominated the premier performances in Formula 2 racing apart from the following:

19 May – SMRC Formula 2 Race, Snetterton, GB – 15 laps, 40.65 miles
Lotus-Climax 11 *Tommy Dickson* 26:55.1, 83.82 mph; PP – n/a; FL – *Dickson*, 1:54.0, 85.58 mph

14 July – Coupe Internationale de Vitesse, Reims-Gueux – 37 laps, 190.92 miles
Ferrari Dino 156 *Maurice Trintignant* 1:40:06.8, 114.39 mph; PP – *Trintignant*; FL – *Brabham's* rear-engined Cooper-Climax

5 October – International Gold Cup, Oulton Park, GB – 50 laps, 138.15 miles
Won by *Brabham's* rear-engined Cooper Climax; PP – n/a; FL – Lotus-Climax 12* *Graham Hill*, 1:53.2, 87.81 mph (*The true Formula 2 front-engined Lotus single-seater producing its first premier performance)

1958

The New Formula 2 season's only front-engined premier performances were as follows:

7 April – Lavant Cup, Goodwood, GB
Lotus-Climax 12 *Graham Hill*, FL – 1:30.2, 95.79 mph

24 May – Crystal Palace Trophy, London, GB
Lotus-Climax 12 *Ivor Bueb* won 15-lap Heat One in 16:04.4, 77.83 mph, set FL – 1:02.4, 80.19 mph

8 June – BRSCC Formula 2 Race, Brands Hatch, GB
Lotus-Climax 12 *Dennis Taylor* in Heat Two set joint FL – 58.2, 76.70 mph

15 June – Pris de Paris, Montlhéry, Paris, F – 15 laps, 57.81 miles
Lotus-Climax 12 *Dennis Taylor* 39:46.8, 94.32 mph; PP – n/a; FL – n/a

5 July – Anerley Trophy, Crystal Palace, London, GB
Ivor Bueb Heat One PP – 1:02.4

27 July – Trophée d'Auvergne, Clermont-Ferrand, F
Lotus-Climax 12 *Ivor Bueb*, FL – 3:56.8, 74.90 mph

4 August – Kent Trophy, Brands Hatch, GB
Lotus-Climax 12s *Cliff Allison* and *Dennis Taylor* shared Heat One FL – 58.2, 76.70 mph

1959

25 April – Gran Premio Siracusa, Sicily, I
Ferrari Dino 156 *Jean Behra*, FL – 1:59.0, 103.52 mph

This was the last premier performance to be achieved by a front-engined car in Formula 2 racing.